The Student and Supervision
in Social Work Education

LIBRARY OF SOCIAL WORK

GENERAL EDITOR: NOEL TIMMS
Lecturer in Social Science and Administration
London School of Economics

The Student and Supervision in Social Work Education

by Priscilla H. Young

Lecturer, School of Social Work
University of Leicester

LONDON

ROUTLEDGE AND KEGAN PAUL

NEW YORK: THE HUMANITIES PRESS

First published 1967
by Routledge and Kegan Paul Ltd
Broadway House, 68-74 Carter Lane
London, E.C.4.

Printed in Great Britain
by Bookprint Limited
Crawley, Sussex

General editor's introduction

The Library of Social Work is designed to meet the needs of students following courses of training for social work. In recent years the number and kinds of training in Britain have increased in an unprecedented way. But there has been no corresponding increase in the supply of text books to cover the growing differentiation of subject matter, nor to respond to the growing spirit of enthusiastic but critical enquiry into the range of subjects relevant for social work. The Library of Social Work will consist of short texts designed to introduce the student to the main features of each topic of enquiry, to the significant theoretical contributions so far made to its understanding, and to some of the outstanding problems. Each volume will suggest ways in which the student might continue his work by further reading.

Since the second half of the nineteenth century, it has been recognised that practice in a social work agency plays an essential part in the education of the social worker. Priscilla Young demonstrates that such practice is more than a simple apprenticeship. She shows clearly the educational content and process of supervision, illustrating her complex subject matter with concrete examples of problems and progress in individual students. She examines the roles of supervisor as teacher, helper and administrator and stresses that field work practice is a course, like other courses, in a professional training programme.

The demand for social workers to accept students for supervision continually increases, and many social workers are called on to both teach and practice in the same job. Social work students should know more about supervision if they are to share in it and increase their skill and knowledge as practitioners. This volume in the Library has thus been designed to illuminate a new aspect of the role of many social workers and to help students understand a method of education which may well prove to be an important contribution to professional training in general.

NOEL TIMMS

Contents

Note

Throughout the text the supervisor is referred to as 'she', and the student as 'he'. In reality, students and supervisors are of both sexes.

I

Education for social work

Education for social work in Great Britain is in a phase of rapid expansion, and opportunities for training are offered to students from a wide variety of educational backgrounds. No large training centres have been established, but courses, each catering for a small number of students, have appeared in many parts of the country, mainly in university social science and extra-mural departments, and in colleges of commerce and technology. All students on these courses undertake field work in social work agencies; many agencies accept students from several different training centres, and supervisors may be asked at different times (and sometimes simultaneously) to undertake the supervision of young students, of older students who have moved into social work from other fields, of graduates, or of students whose educational background has contained little formal academic study.

Basic and professional courses

A distinction must be drawn between these two groups of courses.

Basic courses are those which lead to a degree, or

university certificate in social studies, but which do not claim to provide *training* for social work. Students on such courses may proceed to professional training, or may apply for posts in one of the social work services, but a recent study has shown that in fact many take further training, and employment in quite different fields.[1] Students from basic courses usually have fairly short periods of field work in a number of different agencies.

Professional courses are of several different kinds. Specialised courses are offered by the Home Office Probation and After-care Department, and the Institute of Medical Social Workers, and the majority of psychiatric social workers receive their training on one of the university mental health courses. Courses leading to the award of the Certificate in Social Work are sited in colleges of commerce and technology, where there are sometimes parallel two-year courses leading to the Letter of Recognition in Child Care.

University courses for students who already hold a degree, or certificate in social studies, are of two types. There are one-year courses providing recognised professional qualifications for work in one or more of the main fields of professional social work, i.e. medical social work, probation, child care, psychiatric social work or family casework. These are open to students who hold a degree in the social sciences, or a university certificate in social studies.

There are also courses for graduates in arts or science, which have so far provided training only for students entering the fields of child care or probation. These courses last seventeen months, but there are indications that some universities may decide to vary this pattern, lengthening the course and awarding successful students a higher degree.

This glance at the different courses for social workers is intended only to emphasise the diversity of students sent to social work agencies for supervised field work. An agency which accepts students from only one course will find that each student has his own particular needs, and will make rather different demands on the supervisor. When students are coming from a number of different courses, an even greater flexibility is demanded of both the agency and the individual supervisor if each student is to be provided with the kind of learning experience he needs at the particular point in his professional development.

The place of field work in a course

Professional training of any kind generally includes field work. Students must learn not only *about* the job they will be doing and *how* to carry out professional tasks, but also actually *to do* the job. The first introduction to field work comes early for the student who intends to be a social worker, during or at the end of his basic course, and very near the start of any professional course. Students are required to undertake a certain amount of field work as an integral part of the course, and if it is to be of maximum usefulness to the student, he, his supervisor and his tutor need to see it as such. It is important to stress that field work is one part of a whole course, and not just something 'tacked on' to academic study. Supervisors are often uncertain about the exact purposes of field work placements, and are even less clear about what the course tutor wants the particular student to learn from the placement. In this situation the planning of the student's work cannot be purposeful in terms of his learning. This is not to say that a student will fail to learn from his field work if his supervisor is unsure exactly what the course tutor had in mind when arranging the placement. Fortunately most students are eager for new experiences and do learn much from field work placements anyway. But where there is good co-operative planning between the academic course and the field work agency, there is a better opportunity for the student to learn from both the theoretical teaching and the practical experience, as two interlocking parts of the same course.

The purposes of a field work placement will, of course, vary according to the stage the student has reached in his education. In the early stages, a student is often given several 'observational' placements, which may last for a few weeks, or may be spread over a longer period, during which he spends a day or two each week in the agency. Usually these placements are intended to introduce the student to a social work agency, where he can see at first hand how such agencies function, and where the service offered by this particular agency fits into the pattern of social services in the area. He begins to meet the agency's clients, and he may be able to do some work with them himself. What he observes in specific situations will illustrate and bring to life some of the theoretical knowledge which he is gaining from classes and from his reading in sociology, psychology, social history and other social science subjects which he will be studying. Many students have never come face to face with the social problems and living conditions which they have learnt about in the classroom until they are sent to their first field work placements. In the live situation they also discover their own reactions, which are sometimes startlingly different from what they had expected. Compassion and the desire to help can be overwhelmed by physical disgust at the first sight of a really dirty home; apparent disregard of conventional standards of morality by certain clients may shock and anger.

By the time a student moves into what might be called a professional placement, he will already have had a first sight of what a social worker's job entails, and will have some experience of the workings of the social services. He will have had contact with clients, and will have undertaken some work on his own. The purpose of a professional placement will still in part be to illustrate and to bring to life the theoretical teaching which the student is receiving. It will also provide the opportunity for the student to learn the skills of a professional social worker. Skills cannot be acquired by observation only, or even by sharing in the work of someone who has mastered them: the beginner must learn by doing, and only by competent performance can he prove that he has acquired skill. Through the course of a professional placement, the student has to assume increasing responsibility for his work. His supervisor will carry responsibility for helping him to learn and to increase his skills, but except in very rare instances, the student has to carry responsibility for the actual provision of the agency's services to his clients.

Within the broadly defined purposes of any field work placement, each individual student will have certain things he wants or needs to learn. Part of what he hopes to gain from his placement may be in terms of new experiences: he may want to attend a certain court or committee, to visit a particular institution, or to work with a client of a specific age group. He will also need to consider his aims in terms of his professional development, what aspects of his work he wants to concentrate on, what particular skills he hopes to strengthen. For example, one student may have difficulty in writing clear records and keeping them up to date. Another may find it particularly hard to work with clients who are hostile or critical. A third may tend to expect his clients to move towards a solution to their difficulties at a faster pace than they can manage. The learning of each student will be more purposeful if he and his supervisor have come to some agreement about what he wants to gain from the placement to increase his skill and competence as a social worker. Such learning goals may need to be revised and altered in the course of a placement, but defining them initially does help to provide direction and focus to the student's learning.

Learning the practice of social work

It has become almost a cliché, but it is still true that all effective social work is based on the ability of the worker to establish constructive and meaningful relationships with both his colleagues and the recipients of the service he offers. Only he as a person can do this. He cannot rely solely on learned techniques or on theoretical understanding. The relationship he makes with a client (or with a group of clients) is professional, but it must be honest and genuine, if it is to be an effective milieu for the giving and receiving of help.

The *practice* of social work is an art. The knowledge which supports it is drawn from the social sciences, medicine, and psychiatry, but when the practitioner uses his knowledge to give help to people in trouble, he is practising an art. Good social work practice is creative. The best social workers use their own personalities in helping their clients, bringing into play intuition, imagination, and feelings, as well as knowledge and technical skill.

The social worker in training is therefore involved in learning at several different levels: intellectually, emotionally, and practically.

Theoretical courses, reading, and written work in the academic part of the course will be increasing his knowledge of the dynamics of human behaviour. He will be learning about physical and mental illness, and he will have to consider the functions of the social services and the place of professional social work within them. The course will also include teaching in social work method, (in this country usually casework method, but now with some inclusion of working with groups), and the student must learn to analyse and understand what is involved in helping people in trouble so that he will be able to think methodically about his own social work practice.

A student social worker cannot avoid learning about feelings, his own and other people's. Clients in trouble are likely to be afraid, angry, ashamed, bewildered or distressed, and the people whose job it is to help have feelings of their own too. They are often anxious and uncertain about particular cases, and they can be angry or distressed by the suffering they see. Social work clients may behave unreasonably. They sometimes seem unco-operative and foolish, or just apathetic. Even an understanding of the possible causes of such behaviour cannot always prevent social workers from feeling irritated and frustrated.

The student social worker is also learning to do a job. He is involved in activity of all kinds, not only talking directly to his clients, but making arrangements, writing or dictating letters and reports, using the telephone, co-operating with other services in the community, attending courts, committees and staff meetings. Social workers, particularly in the public social services, have much to accomplish, and are often short of time, so the student must learn to organise his work, and to select priorities when under pressure.

To summarise, the social work student is involved in learning skill in the practice of an art, which requires the backing and control of theoretical knowledge and technical understanding to bring his performance to a professional level. In the process of learning he cannot avoid involvement as a whole person, being, knowing, feeling and doing. This is a demanding training in many ways, but one which can also be enjoyable, exciting and rewarding.

Stages of learning

In field work, the focus of attention is on the acquisition of skills, that is, learning actually to do, as well as *what* to do and *how* to do it. In acquiring any skill, the beginner's attention is taken up with the actual motions he is performing, and it is only with practice and increased confidence that he can perform the operation without conscious thought: the skill has then become 'part of him'.

Over twenty years ago, Bertha Reynolds[2] defined the stages in mastering skill in the practice of social work. If a field work supervisor is to be sensitive to the needs of each student, she needs to be aware that all of us go through stages in our learning, not steadily and with clear lines of demarcation between one stage and the next, but often jerkily, meeting obstacles, slipping back in some areas, though always moving forward. Good teaching in any field has to be related to the needs and stage of development of the learner, as well as to the goals aimed at, and the stages of learning which Bertha Reynolds defined are useful for supervisors in thinking about their students (and could also be applied to the supervisor's own learning in the skills of supervision). Her headings are used, but for the interpretations the author takes full responsibility.

1. *The stage of acute consciousness of self*. Most social workers will be able to recall the paralysing awareness of their own lack of knowledge and experience when they first had to knock on a front door (hoping devoutly that there would be no one at home). This 'stage fright' is not confined to beginning students, but can re-occur disconcertingly

in later years in the face of new demands, such as public speaking, teaching, or even supervising. Students at this stage are lacking the confidence which only experience can provide, and each will react to insecurity in the way which is most characteristic for him. A few will appear over-confident, others very apprehensive. Some will talk too much, others retreat into silence. Many students do in fact manage their introduction to social work practice without any acute anxiety, but there can hardly be one who has not felt nervous about his first interviews and visits, and many a student has been grateful for the background security and encouragement provided by an understanding supervisor.

2. *The stage of sink-or-swim adaptation.* Assuming that contacts with clients in the early stages of training have been chosen so that the student has been able to manage them with a reasonable degree of success, his anxiety about his own inadequacy has a chance to diminish, and he is likely to be able to relax and be more his usual self. If at the same time he can feel that his supervisor will protect him from situations in which he could make disastrous mistakes, he can begin to be more spontaneous in his response to clients. At this stage students should not be asked to be self-critical or to analyse too closely what they are doing. The learner's attention at this stage of learning is still focused on the actual carrying out of his tasks. He will have a fair idea of whether he is managing well or badly, but while the 'doing' is still so new, it will take up all his energy. A student who is asked to become too self-aware before he has gained a reasonable amount of confidence through experience is likely to be thrown into confusion. While it is usually all too easy to reduce a student's self-confidence, it is sometimes very difficult to restore it once it has been shaken. This is not to suggest that a

supervisor should be uncritical. Students should be encouraged to think about what they are doing, and about the people and the problems they are meeting. But excessive introspective thinking at an early stage of learning can hinder, not help, a student's progress.

3. *The stage of understanding the situation without power to control one's own activity in it.* By this third stage the student has gained enough security in practice to study the situation and his own part in it. In retrospect, and sometimes at the time, he can grasp what is happening between him and his client in an interview. He becomes aware of what is not being said, as well as what is said. He will see when a client is trying to manipulate him, and he can begin to assess where he has been helpful, or unhelpful. At this stage he can understand what to do and how to do it. Sometimes, but not always, he can put his understanding into practice. The power to control his professional activity has not fully caught up with his understanding, a condition which can be very frustrating. No newly-trained worker can expect to have progressed beyond this third stage in learning – indeed which of us ever gets past it completely? But to have reached it does give a basis for continued learning, even if in employment there may not be many opportunities for supervision or consultation.

Bertha Reynolds suggests that there are two further stages of learning, that of *relative mastery*, when one can both understand and control one's activity, and finally, the stage of *learning to teach the art one has mastered* – this is what beginning field-work supervisors are learning to do, and the following chapters are concerned with different aspects of this task.

REFERENCES

(1) RODGERS, BARBARA N. 'The Careers of Social Studies Students', Occasional Papers on Social Administration No. 11, The Codicote Press, 1964.
(2) REYNOLDS, BERTHA C. *Learning and Teaching in the Practice of Social Work*, Farrar and Rinehart, New York, 1942, Chapter 7. (Reprinted by Russell and Russell, New York, 1965.)

II

The responsibilities of the student supervisor

It is only of recent years, with the expansion of vocational training for social work, that the specific and specialised task of the supervisor of field work has come to be recognised. It used to be assumed that the way to train a student was to attach him to an experienced social worker who gave him a certain amount of instruction, answered his questions, and supervised his work on an apprenticeship basis. On this assumption, still held in some quarters, the only qualification necessary for a supervisor was that she should be reasonably competent and knowledgeable in her own field of practice; if, in addition, she held a recognised professional qualification, so much the better. Many students did, and still do, learn a great deal from supervisors selected only by virtue of their experience and their interest in training, and nothing which follows is in any way intended to belittle the value of what they have given to social work education.

Reference has been made in the preceding chapter to theoretical and field work teaching as interlocking sections of a total course, so that the student is able to apply his academic knowledge in practice, and to use his field work experience to illuminate the theory he is being taught. If a close connection between the theoretical and practical aspects of the course is to be maintained, the supervisor must be regarded as part of the teaching team, and her function seen as an educative one. The student has to learn the skills of a social worker, and although skill has to be acquired by doing, the student's experiences must be planned, and he needs help in learning from them. This after all is the essence of teaching – providing learning experiences and helping the learner to make use of them. From the point of view of the organiser of any course, then, the supervisor is the teacher who is responsible for giving the student a 'course' in field work.

The supervisor's responsibility as an educator

To make it clear that supervision in social work training has something more to it than straightforward instruction, the heading to this section describes the supervisor as an educator.

1. *Planning.* In an issue of *Case Conference* devoted to training, a report of a discussion on student supervision includes a remark made by one of the participants: 'It is more important for you to have a plan than for it to be a perfect one. If he (the student) is not to feel his time is being wasted, he needs to be certain you are interested in his education.'[1] This is a statement which might be pondered by all supervisors. The experiences and work chosen will depend upon the stage of the student's development, the purpose of the placement, and of course, the work available in the agency at the time. The programme selected should not give the student a host of disconnected experiences, but should try to provide a 'course' which has a recognisable entity and which he can relate to his total learning.

For example, a student whose placement is intended to provide him with an introduction to the work of the particular agency, will spend some time with the social workers, and may attend committee meetings and case conferences. He can also widen the picture, by reading a few cases specially chosen to show particular aspects of the agency's work, or to illustrate work undertaken in co-operation with other services. In discussion with the student, the supervisor will want to be sure that he has a sufficient grasp of the function, structure, and administration of the agency to be able to put into context the various aspects of its work which he has been shown. If the student is training to work in another service, he might be encouraged to analyse the similarities and differences between this agency and the service in which he will be employed.

Students placed for much longer periods of field work also need to have a 'course' planned for them. For example, a probation trainee in his final placement needs to have experience of as many sides of the work of a probation officer as possible, including sufficient acquaintance with the legal aspects of the job. He needs a certain degree of technical 'know-how' before he takes up a post as a trained officer, if he is to be able to carry the job efficiently and with confidence. As mentioned in the previous chapter, he will also have some things to work on which are specific to his particular needs as a social worker in training, and his supervisor will need to plan work experiences for him which will give him the opportunity to learn and to progress as a caseworker.

2. *A climate for learning.* Another part of the supervisor's responsibility as an educator is to create a climate for the student which allows him to develop and to learn as a social worker. The practical arrangements which need to be made for students in a social work agency are dealt

with in the next chapter, and while these can help to provide a suitable environment in which to learn, what is even more important is the relationship which is established between the supervisor and each individual student. Students need to be at ease with their supervisors as far as possible, not to be afraid, and to receive plenty of encouragement, but they also need to know where their performance could be improved. Students undergoing professional training have been known to express a wish that their supervisors would be a little more astringent in their comments, once student and supervisor have got to know each other, and a helpful and supportive relationship has been established. If a student is confident that his supervisor is concerned about him as a person, and is genuinely interested in helping him to learn, he can take the discouragements and difficulties which arise and use them constructively, supported and stimulated by the relationship with his supervisor: the good student *wants* the constructive criticism which will help him learn.

Expanding training programmes mean more field work supervisors, and many social workers are under pressure to move into student supervision before they feel ready for it. Others, who were trained some years ago, feel that the content of the academic teaching today is so different from what they themselves were given, that their students must know a great deal more than they do. This situation is probably inevitable in a rapidly expanding and young profession, where training is not standardised, and where those who are responsible for setting up training programmes are still to some extent experimenting. It may make unfair demands on some supervisors, but however unsure of her own capabilities, any social worker with experience (and supervisors do have more experience than their students, either in years or in training) *can*, if she is willing to give the time and energy, provide the right climate for a student to learn. She can provide support, encouragement and interest, she can give of her own experience, and she can stimulate the student to think purposefully about his work, and to draw on his own theoretical knowledge.

3. *Teaching*. Academic courses, however carefully planned, never do succeed in meeting all the needs of all the students, at the right time for each one. In their field work, students will have to try and understand adolescents while they are still learning about personality development in infancy; they will meet problems of mental illness before they have had any teaching in psychiatry; they will have to discover the law relating to adoption procedure before the lecturer has reached the subject. From time to time supervisors have to assume responsibility for some direct teaching, to provide a student with sufficient information in a particular area, to enable him to tackle his work in the agency.

There are occasions when knowledge is simply lacking, but there are many others when the student needs help in relating what he knows in theory to the actual situation which he faces. The supervisor who can resist the temptation to spell out the connection between theory and practice, and can help the student to discover it for himself, is teaching in a way which is more likely to ensure that the student really learns from the experience, than if her approach is didactic.

4. *Personal feelings*. It has already been suggested that students who are training for social work are undergoing an educational process which involves them in being, feeling, knowing and doing. What has been said so far about the supervisor's responsibilities as an educator has been mainly concerned with the knowing and doing aspects. What about the being and feeling?

In this country most of us are brought up to control our feelings; children are exhorted not to cry, to be 'good losers', not to show fear, they are often even expected to take punishment or frustration cheerfully. We express admiration for courage which is shown in refusing to give way to grief, and to see an adult, particularly a man, weep in public, except under quite extraordinary stress, is an embarrassing experience for the onlooker. The expression of strong emotion is normally something private, and if we lose control of our emotions in public we tend to feel ashamed. Yet even if we succeed in suppressing or controlling feelings, this does not eliminate them, nor, on the other hand, can we produce a feeling reaction to order.

To be a good social worker, one has to care about people, and caring brings other feelings in its train : anger, anxiety, disgust, dislike, as well as liking, concern, pleasure, and sympathy. The division implied in that last sentence illustrates another common attitude to feelings: some are 'good', and others are 'bad', and somehow we feel we should be able to rid ourselves of our 'bad' feelings, and cultivate the 'good' ones. Whatever our attitudes to our own and other people's feelings, and whatever we think we ought to do about them, feelings exist, whether they are acknowledged or not: the adjectives 'good' or 'bad', 'constructive' or 'destructive', are perhaps more appropriately used to describe the attitudes and behaviour which result from feelings, rather than the feelings themselves.

The area of feeling must be taken into consideration from the very beginning of professional education, if the student is to develop that sensitive awareness of feelings which is so essential to good social work practice. Intuitive understanding of other people involves being able to feel with them; not to feel *as* they do, which would mean being completely caught up in their experience, but to be sufficiently sensitive to allow their emotions to touch one. To be free to feel with other people in this way, the social worker has also to be aware of his or her own feeling reactions. If this awareness is not developed, there may be a danger of the social worker confusing his own feelings with those of his client.

Students embarking on training for social work cannot avoid meeting people and situations which evoke personal reactions, and they have to find ways to deal with their emotions which are tolerable for themselves, and as far as possible, acceptable to others. Strong feelings can be uncomfortable and disturbing, but intending social workers often pick up the idea that 'being involved' is incompatible with professional attitudes, and may be reluctant to admit to personal feelings. Part of the responsibility of a supervisor as an educator is to be aware of a student's feeling reaction to his field work experiences, so that he does not 'insulate' himself against his own or his clients' feelings. From the very beginning of training he must be helped to sharpen his sensitivity, not to blunt it by trying to eliminate his feelings in a professional situation. One cannot always assume that a student does not wish to talk about his own feelings because he does not take the initiative in doing so, and if the supervisor provides no opportunity for him to discuss personal reactions, he may conclude that they have no place in professional social work.

Social work students know *about* social problems, about physical and mental illness, poor living conditions, delinquency, illegitimacy and so on. They probably come with a helpful attitude to people in trouble, more ready to pity than to condemn, and with at least a beginning intellectual understanding of some of the causes of problems in human relationships. For some students it is not difficult to be tolerant and understanding in theory, though for others it is less easy to accept what may be very different attitudes, from those they have known in their own families, to such problems as out-of-wedlock pregnancy, drunkenness, and indebtedness, to suggest but a few. In any case intellectual tolerance and understanding is likely to come first, and is not the same thing as being able to feel, and to be, tolerant in a 'real life' situation. It is possible, for instance, to appreciate that a mother whose own childhood was bleak and loveless, and who felt inferior and unwanted, may find it very difficult, if not impossible, to treat her own children with love and gentleness, and to give them the security which they need. It is a different matter to be involved in an actual situation where it is plain that a child's troubles are caused by his mother's attitude to him, her lack of understanding, perhaps her rejection or actual ill-treatment. Even experienced social workers are apt to react with anger in a situation of this kind, and to identify themselves with the child; how much more likely that a student, whatever his age, may find that he has strong personal feelings which he must come to recognise and to understand, if he is to be able to help not only children, but also their parents! It is not unprofessional to have personal reactions: what *is* unprofessional is to be so controlled by personal feelings and reactions that they hinder the effective carrying out of the job to be done. Students have therefore to learn from experience something about their own emotional responses to the situations and people they meet professionally, for once personal feelings are acknowledged and understood they are more easily controlled and used.

Professional training for social work does not aim to produce an insulated, 'clinical' practitioner, who remains impartial, kind, and largely impersonal in professional relationships, but a trained and skilled worker, who can allow himself to have feelings, and is not afraid of a controlled involvement in professional relationships.

The supervisor's responsibility as a helper

The background and training of the majority of student supervisors is that of social work, not of education, and until very recently many have had to begin supervising without any preparation other than their own experiences as students. In these circumstances it sometimes happens that a supervisor is either insufficiently aware of the inherent differences between teacher/student and case-worker/client relationships, or she tends to be so conscious that she must not treat her student as a client, that she fails to use her experience and understanding of people's reactions to stress to help the student to learn. Extremes in either direction are likely to cause difficulties; a student who feels himself to be under 'treatment' for personal problems which he may or may not acknowledge, is likely to resent and to resist the supervisor's efforts to 'help', while the student whose supervisor seems unwilling to help him to deal with the parts of himself which hinder his learning, is also likely to feel that he is not getting what he needs from supervision.

The purpose of any field work placement is to further the student's learning as an intending social worker; the primary task of the supervisor is, therefore, to help the student to learn, which will inevitably involve her in accepting responsibility for helping the student to deal with difficulties which block progress. In this sense a supervisor has to be prepared to take a helping role and she will draw on her knowledge and experience as a social worker to do so. Yet she must hold to her function as an educator, and not allow herself to treat her student as if he were a client.

Clients come to social workers because they have problems which they cannot manage alone, and the function of the social worker is to try and help them to find a way to solve, or to mitigate their difficulties. Students come to learn to be social workers, and the assumption must be that they are sufficiently stable and healthy to be able to deal with problems in ordinary living, without calling on professional help. Of course, this does not mean that students are necessarily without conflicts or difficulties in their personal lives, but the relationship which the student has with his supervisor can easily become predominantly therapeutic rather than educational, if the supervisor becomes too involved in helping the student to resolve personal conflicts.

It needs to be said here that it is sometimes the student who tries to manoeuvre the supervisor into the role of a therapist, seeking to use her help to explore his personal difficulties and conflicts. In so far as these difficulties affect his performance as a social worker, and impede his learning, it may be relevant to discuss them, but again keeping clearly in view the fact that the relationship between supervisor and student must remain that of teacher and learner. The concern of the supervisor is to help the student to see where his own anxieties, attitudes, and personal difficulties are preventing him from giving the best service to his clients. Some students, once they see what it is that is blocking progress, need no further help and can deal with it themselves. Others may be unable to understand just what is causing the problem, and will need more help in tracing its origin. From time to time students reveal personal problems which they cannot manage alone, and it then becomes the task of the supervisor to co-operate with the course tutor in helping the student to seek professional advice outside the educational setting.

Students vary considerably in the amount of help which

they need in learning, but all students do have to make adjustments, and many have to come to terms with aspects of their own personalities which they find difficult to face. The experience of learning to become a social worker involves the student in a process of change, and while change can be stimulating and exciting, it can also provoke anxiety and resistance. At first sight it may appear strange that students who have chosen to become social workers, and who often have a great deal at stake as far as their future careers are concerned, should resist learning, but the situation in which they find themselves, involved in learning a professional skill in which they are asked to know, to feel, and to do, does make demands beyond those experienced in most other learning situations.

There are three main sources from which difficulties may arise for students; these are from his feelings about being dependent, from his own life experiences, and from his anxieties about involvement and detachment.

1. *Dependence.* Feelings about dependence are liable to arise from the role of student in a field work setting. The young student who comes straight to professional education, with or without a university qualification, has not had very long to establish himself as an adult, independent of his parental home, and many have not completely left behind the conflicts of adolescence. Young students may feel that they had achieved a degree of freedom and responsibility for their own actions which is now being curtailed: in their field work they are required to do things in a certain way, and often at a prescribed time, and there are certain situations in which they are required to consult the supervisor before making a decision. Sometimes young students, full of enthusiasm and energy, feel that they are, as it were, being put back into the nursery, and they resent what they regard as 'red tape'.

For the older person, the role of a student is not without its difficulties either. People who have carried responsibility and who have gained a measure of adult competence and assurance, often find it hard to return to a situation where they are learners, and in which they may feel uncertain or helpless. They may even find that they have supervisors who are younger than they are. For any student, having to submit to the authority, and superior knowledge and experience of a supervisor, can be a very difficult situation arousing strong feelings. The student may react by taking too much responsibility on himself, or by avoiding discussions with the supervisor; again he may go to the opposite extreme and rely on the supervisor, almost to the point of refusing to think for himself at all. Until recently the majority of both social work students and supervisors were women, except in the probation service, where the reverse is true, and where, with some exceptions, tutor officers traditionally supervised students of their own sex. With a greater number of men entering all branches of social work, and with the need to use good supervisors as fully as possible, it is becoming increasingly common to find men supervising women students, and vice versa. Women students are usually less concerned about being supervised by a man, but a male student does not always as happily accept a woman supervisor. There is no good reason why students should always have a supervisor of their own sex, and indeed they often gain a great deal from working with a supervisor of the opposite sex, but supervisors do need to be aware that the student may have some feelings about the situation, and be ready to let him (or her) say so. In any situation where there seem to be difficulties, some discussion of the particular problems involved for this student in the position of learner will often help the student to deal with his feelings more easily, and free him to concentrate his energies on learning, instead of resisting being in a partially dependent position.

2. *Past life experiences.* A second source of problems with which the student may need his supervisor's help is his own life experiences, or as Charlotte Towle puts it, 'the persistence of the past in the present'.[2] A student, like anybody else, has been influenced by his experiences, and by the important relationships he has made. He has probably incorporated the attitudes and values of people he has loved or admired, and he will have developed his own particular method of dealing with stressful situations. As a social worker he is being asked to use himself as a whole person, and he cannot avoid bringing, as part of himself, attitudes, reactions and ways of behaving which stem from his own past. Much of what he is and has learned can be used to help clients, but equally there may be parts of his past experience which prevent him from helping.

For example: A beginning student in a medical social work setting quickly overcame her initial shyness and was able to relate warmly to patients, giving them the support and understanding they needed, and helping them to make plans towards solving practical problems. At first the student found it difficult to allow patients to reveal their anxieties and distresses to her, but with her supervisor's help, she was able to see that patients sometimes need to talk about their fears and doubts, whether in relation to their own illnesses or to their family relationships. Sometimes it might even be a relief to a patient to be allowed to be upset. Her ability to help patients developed markedly as she became able to let them show their feelings, but she still seemed unable to allow patients' relatives to reveal their distress and anxieties. People who were ill had an 'excuse' for revealing their feelings, but apparently relatives had not. The supervisor suggested that the student should try and think about why she reacted in this way, and gradually it emerged that the student's own family did not talk much about how they felt, and that each member had found other ways of giving vent to emotions. Some years previously a close relative had been seriously ill, and the rest of the family had gone through the period of anxiety scarcely revealing even to each other the fear and distress they were all feeling. Controlling and concealing emotions was the way that this particular family had dealt with this stress. The student carried over into a professional situation her own personal expectations of how relatives of a seriously ill patient might be expected to behave, and until she was helped to see what she was doing, could not encourage, or even permit, them to behave in any other way.

Present experiences or demands of many different kinds can arouse emotional responses which belonged to the past; once a student is able to see that his response to certain situations is preventing him from helping his clients effectively, his wish to be of help to them will often provide a sufficient stimulus for him to risk trying to respond in a different way. Some students are more readily open to learning from new relationships and experiences, while others may cling longer to responses and attitudes learned in the past, now inappropriate in the role of a professional social worker.

3. *Involvement and detachment.* Earlier in this chapter there has been some discussion of the involvement of a student's own feelings in the practice of social work, and what follows here is really a different aspect of the same topic, finding a balance between giving and withholding, between involvement and detachment. Social workers have to be able to give of themselves fully and freely when the occasion demands, but it is also important for them to be

able to withhold, in the interests of both those they serve and themselves.

The need and desire to give is strong in students of social work. They want to give their sympathy and concern for people in trouble, their knowledge and skills; they want to give both of the richness of their own lives, and of the understanding they have gained from the hurts and frustrations they may have experienced. Yet as students in field work, they are often faced with situations and people who make demands beyond what they feel they are capable of giving. Such a situation is likely to arouse the student's anxiety about his ability to tolerate the personal demands which social work will make upon him.

Helping other people does take something from the helper, and sometimes students are anxious lest their personal resources may somehow run dry if too many demands are made upon them. There are the occasions when the support and understanding of a supervisor can help a student to go on rather than withdraw from a situation which is being particularly demanding, and in so doing he may begin to find that the normal demands of a social work job can be tolerated. Giving of oneself is exhausting, and refreshment and relaxation are essential, but as any experienced social worker will testify, the capacity for using oneself in helping people in trouble develops with use. It is not a matter of having a resource which will eventually be used up, but students will only be able to accept this fully by experiencing it in themselves.

Students striving to find a balance between involvement and detachment tend to swing between the two extremes. Many a student has had his sympathy and concern so aroused by a client, whom he very much wants to help, that he finds himself identified with the client to such an extent that he is viewing the problems, and feeling about them, in

much the same way as the client does. It is now more difficult for him to help this client, and, for his own sake as well,
he must learn to protect himself against the kind of personal
involvement which exhausts emotional energy and, in the
long run, decreases his ability to give professional help.
After going through an experience of this kind (and many
potentially good social workers do) a student may for a
time be wary of involvement, but if he is able to learn from
his experiences, he will gradually find what might be
called a balance in identification. He will acquire an acceptance of himself as a social worker, with a defined role in
relation to his clients, and to the community in which they
both live, and in so doing he will have to accept the
difference between them. A social worker is the same as
his client, in the sense that they are both human beings,
with all that that implies. But if a social worker is to be
able to give help, he must accept that his knowledge, his
skill, and his professional identity as a social worker makes
him different from his clients – different, not better or
worse. This difference does not prevent him from feeling
with his client, but it does helpfully prevent him from the
over-identification, the uncontrolled 'giving' of himself,
which reduces his capacity to help his client, and exhausts
him as a person.

Among the students who come for training in social
work, one finds those whose difficulties lie in the direction
of reluctance to be involved personally in their work. There
seem to be two interrelated aspects to this particular difficulty; one is the student's fear that he may find that he has
little to give as a person, and therefore it is safer to stay
strictly 'professional' with his clients; the other is the
student's anxieties about what it will do to him as a person if
he allows himself to be involved in other people's troubles.
Either way, giving is experienced as 'dangerous', and the

student is likely to withhold himself from becoming involved. No one can 'talk' a student into believing that he has something to offer as a person, but he would not have been selected for training, if he was not thought to have something to give, and this knowledge, together with his supervisor's encouragement, may help him to risk involving himself. The plunge once taken, most students find themselves having to admit that they are able to offer something from their own personalities to their clients, in addition to their growing professional knowledge. The student who resists involvement mainly for fear of what it will do to him is often afraid of not being able to keep himself sufficiently separate from his clients, and afraid, too, lest the experience will change him as a person. Learning does involve change, and in order to learn to become a professional social worker, a student will go through experiences which he will have to allow to touch him personally, if he is to move forward. For most students their sincere concern for their clients, and their wish to help, provide sufficient motivation for them to risk some involvement, once they have been helped to see that this is really the only way they can either learn, or help other people.

The practice of social work brings students (and particularly the younger ones) face to face with problems and experiences of life, some of which they might never meet if they had chosen another career, and others which they would be more likely to encounter in their personal lives in later years. In each situation, however unfamiliar it may be to him, the student is asked to use his knowledge and sympathy, to try to understand this particular person's problems, and to give help towards coming to terms with them. As the student's experience grows, so does his understanding of human behaviour at all stages of life, and, for the young student particularly, it grows beyond his years. He may feel as if he has grown an old head on young shoulders: he has come into contact with situations which his contemporaries in other jobs have never experienced, and he cannot prevent his growing insight into human behaviour spilling over into his personal relationships. This is not necessarily an uncomfortable experience, but every student has to find, in his personal life too, a balance between giving and withholding. He cannot be a social worker to everyone he meets who needs help. Neither can he always refuse to listen or to help, outside the professional situation. The student's personal life is not the direct concern of his supervisor, but it is as well to be aware that students are usually having to make some adjustments in this sphere too.

The supervisor's responsibility as an administrator

In order to stress the supervisor's responsibilities as educator and helper to the student, these two aspects have been considered first, but with no intention of implying that the supervisor's role as an administrator is in any way less important. As well as being a student supervisor, she is also a practising social worker, with responsibilities and a defined function within the agency. She may have a sizeable caseload of her own, and/or carry responsibility for the work of other staff. Whatever the exact definition of her responsibility, as a member of the agency staff she allocates work to the student to carry out on behalf of the agency.

The work which the student undertakes is not given to him solely for the purpose of providing him with material on which to learn. It is a part of the service which the particular agency offers to clients, whose right to expect competent service must be safeguarded. Beginning students may not carry full responsibility for work with a client or family, but those who have reached the stage of professional training will carry a small caseload of their own, and will be expected to work with their clients in accordance with the agency's policies and practice. Statutory regulations must be observed, records must be kept up to date, other people concerned, such as doctors, teachers, and workers in other agencies, may have to be kept informed of developments, and reports may have to be made to committees or courts. Above all, the client must be given the service which it is the agency's function to offer, and it is the supervisor's responsibility to see that the student gives it. While having regard to the fact that he is a learner, she must hold the student accountable for the work he undertakes on behalf of the agency, and the fact that he *is* a learner, and may be finding parts of the work difficult, cannot entirely excuse him from responsibility. This is a necessary part of the student's learning, and it is better for him to learn what it means to accept responsibility for his own work, while he has the support of a supervisor, rather than to meet it as something new when he is employed.

The combination of teacher and administrator in the one person of the supervisor can be a positive aid to the student's learning. For example, a student may find endless good reasons for not arranging an interview about which he feels apprehensive; the supervisor will discuss it with him, to try to help him to come to terms with his anxiety, but eventually she may be able to help him most by simply requiring him to undertake the interview, in her role as administrator. There comes a point when discussion gets one no further, and it is something of a relief to be held to doing the job one may not avoid. It need hardly be said that the supervisor should be satisfied that the task to be undertaken is within the competence of the student.

In safeguarding the interests of clients, the supervisor is also protecting the student from his own inexperience.

There are occasions when students resent the supervisor's control over their work, but generally speaking it is a reassurance to know that supervisors will not permit them to become involved in situations where their inexperience could be harmful. One of the common fears of beginning students is that they may hurt the clients whom they want to help, and they need to feel that they will be protected from doing this.

As an administrator the supervisor is in a position to help the student look realistically at the agency, its functioning and policies. Because she is part of it and identified with it, she will be able to help the student to identify himself with the agency, for the time he is working in it, enabling him to see where policies and procedures might be improved (for no agency is perfect), and, if necessary, preventing him at the same time from projecting on to the agency faults which lie in his own work.

To summarise the responsibilities of a student supervisor: she is a member of the staff of an agency, which offers services to clients as its primary function, and it is her responsibility to see that the standard of service is not lower because the work is being undertaken by students. In relation to her students she combines the roles of administrator, teacher, and helper, and her defined task is to provide for them a 'course' in social work practice which will develop their skills as professional social workers.

REFERENCES

(1) 'The Supervisor's View of the Beginning Phase of Casework – A Symposium', *Case Conference*, Vol. 9, No. 9, March 1963.
(2) TOWLE, CHARLOTTE, 'The Place of Help in Supervision', *The Social Service Review*, Vol. XXXVII, No. 4, December 1963.

III

A structure for teaching and learning

The agency, the student, and the supervisor

A student supervisor is part of the educational team of lecturers, tutors and other field work supervisors who come into contact with each student. She does not bear total responsibility for the student's education; over his period of training he will be taught by a number of different people, and at any given moment he is likely to be in contact with at least one member of the educational body which is responsible for his whole course, as well as his field work supervisor.

1. *The staff and the student.* So also in the agency, the supervisor is not the only person who influences the student, or from whom he learns, even when she is specially appointed to be responsible for a student unit. The student's placement is with the agency, not just with the supervisor, and he will learn from other agency staff, from the structure and administration of the office, from his supervisor's attitude to it, and from the position and status of his supervisor as a member of the staff. For the time that he is a student, he is one of the agency's workers, if only a part-time one: he undertakes his allotted portion of the agency's work, he uses the help of the clerical and

administrative staff, and, if only to a limited extent, he represents the agency to the outside world.

If a student is to learn to become a social worker, he must be introduced to all aspects of his future role: he must be skilled in dealing with his clients, but the service he can give to them will be less effective if he cannot also maintain good relationships with colleagues, courts, committees, and workers in other disciplines. However reluctant to be involved, the total staff has to accept students who are placed for training in the agency, and the student's experiences and opportunities for learning will be much greater if he is readily accepted. In an agency where a student is welcome, he has the opportunity to experience what it is like to be a social worker: he is able to attend staff meetings, to present reports to a court or committee, to put forward his opinion at case conferences, or to discuss a client with workers from other disciplines. With the guidance of his supervisor, he learns how to use administrative machinery and how to present a situation to a senior staff member from whom he must obtain a decision. He has direct dealings with social workers on the staff, and with clerical and other workers, and if he finds any difficulty in co-operating with them, his supervisor can help him to find ways of handling the situation better.

A supervisor who finds herself training students, without the positive co-operation of the whole agency behind her, is at a considerable disadvantage when it comes to giving the student opportunity to experience what it means to be a professional social worker in relation to colleagues, lay committee members, magistrates, and the many other people with whom a social worker must co-operate inside as well as outside the agency.

2. *Work for the student.* The co-operation of the whole agency staff is also needed to ensure that work is available

for students. In several settings, it has been the practice until recently to expect the supervisor to allocate work to her student from her own caseload, but if a supervisor has students in rapid succession, or if she has several students simultaneously, she alone cannot provide them with sufficient work without carrying an impossibly large caseload herself. In addition, it would be difficult, if not impossible, to protect clients from having a new worker every time there was a change of student. The only way to ensure that students have sufficient work, and that clients are not too much 'used', is to accept that all social workers on the staff must 'lend' cases for students.

Preparing for a student

1. *Staff and student reactions.* When considering the practical arrangements which have to be made for students in an agency, the supervisor should be aware both of the impact students have on an agency, and the possible reactions of a new student at the beginning of his placement.

Anyone who has supervised students, at whatever stage of training, has usually found the experience stimulating and interesting. Students demand information, and question the reasons for procedures that experienced workers take for granted; they compel supervisors to look again at their own practice, and to explain what they are about, and why. They may be critical of what they see, or they may be enthusiastic about aspects of the agency's work which the workers themselves have long ceased to notice, but whatever their reactions, students bring with them a fresh viewpoint. This can be stimulating, though it can also be disturbing and threatening, particularly to workers whose own training seems remote. In asking for the co-operation of other workers, a supervisor has to be aware that, for older workers particularly, close contact with students may be viewed with some apprehension. A worker who is asked to hand over some of her clients to students, for the period of the placement, is even more vulnerable. The work that she has done is revealed to the student and to the supervisor, and there is always the possibility that the student's work may alter the situation, in such a way that it seems more difficult for the original worker when the case is returned. An even more threatening situation arises where a student accomplishes more with a particular client than the social worker herself has been able to. An awareness of the possible reactions of colleagues to students ensures that a supervisor does all that she can to anticipate the difficulties, so the the student's placement will be of maximum usefulness to him, and as easy and, if possible, rewarding to the other staff involved.

Social workers who have become familiar with the setting in which they work sometimes forget how alarming it (and they) can appear to a newcomer. Local authority and probation offices are busy places where workers are often working under pressure, and perhaps dealing with unexpected crises, so that the general impression is usually one of activity. The whole atmosphere of a hospital may be strange to someone who has neither worked in one, nor been a patient, and the air of quiet efficiency behind closed doors, which pervades some child guidance clinics, can be equally alarming to someone coming into it for the first time.

To a student, social workers have an air of competence, they deal with other people's troubles without appearing to be worried by them, and in most situations they seem to know what to do. However, social workers may also upset students by the way they talk among themselves, because they sometimes sound as if they did not care about their clients, and they may laugh about situations which, to the student, appear more tragic than comic. A supervisor needs to be sensitive to a student's reaction to the general atmosphere of the agency, and to the people he meets in it, and if necessary must help him to look at it realistically, and to understand, for example, that people are sometimes flippant in the face of tragedy, to protect themselves from the distress they would otherwise feel.

The supervisor has to be able to view her employing agency objectively, while remaining identified with it, so that when necessary she can allow the student to discuss it, without feeling she is being disloyal to her colleagues if she agrees with some of his criticisms. In allowing him to be critical, the supervisor can also help the student think constructively about how a social worker may try to improve the service which his agency offers to clients.

2. *Practical arrangements.* Careful planning of the practical arrangements for students does much to save wear and tear on supervisor, student, and the rest of the agency staff. A student needs a corner of his own: somewhere that belongs to him for the time he is in the agency, where he can go whenever he is in the office. He should have a desk and chair of his own, access to a telephone, and to a room where he can interview his clients without interruption. If he is going to be with the agency for more than a very short time, arrangements have to be made for him to have his letters and records typed.

When a new student (or worker) arrives at an agency he has an enormous amount of information to absorb all at once. He cannot possibly remember everything he is told, and if some of the information is written down for him to refer to, it will save him from having to ask endless questions of busy people. Once prepared, a folder containing information about the agency can be used for successive students, and will only have to be kept up to date. A list of the names of all the agency staff, the positions they hold, where they can be found, a map of the area (or where to obtain one), a sample set of the forms most commonly in use in the agency, written instructions about agency procedure, and any regular fixtures such as courts, committees and staff meetings, are fixed items of information which help to give a new student some pegs on which to hang the knowledge he is trying to absorb about this new setting.

A new student needs to be taken round and introduced to all the staff, on his first day if possible, so that they know who he is, even if he does not remember all of them. Clerical and administrative staff who are willing to be involved can do much to help a new student settle into the agency. They can explain filing and record systems, and sometimes they can be much more reassuring and easy to approach than the supervisor, who is still an unknown quantity, and may seem a rather awe-inspiring figure. The help that clerical staff can give is particularly evident in small agencies, where there are only a few social workers, and probably just one student at a time.

Where they are several students in the same agency, they may all share a room, and gain a good deal of support from each other, besides having opportunities to discuss the work they are doing among themselves. Students often feel that they benefit from sharing an office with a permanent member of the staff, for a time at least, and can get the feeling of the agency, and a sense of someone else's work: others prefer to have a quiet corner of their own, where they can work without interruptions. There are things to be said for each of these ways of accommodating students in an office. One point which perhaps needs making in this connection, is that it will probably be something of a strain for student and supervisor, if they have to share an office for any length of time. Neither really wants to be continually under the eye of the other, and it is probably easier for all concerned if separate accommodation can be made available for students who are going to be in the agency for several months.

Students always want to know how they should introduce themselves to their clients, and how to sign their letters and reports, so this needs immediate clarification with a new student, and with any other members of the staff who have not been concerned with students before. A student sent to the agency for a short placement can probably most simply be introduced as a student, but it seems more appropriate to give a slightly different status to those who have a longer period of field work, or are further advanced in their training. To the ear of the general public, the word 'student' tends to convey a suggestion of youth, inexperience, and irresponsibility, and while social work students at the stage of professional training often are young, and relatively inexperienced, they are rarely irresponsible, and they already have the beginnings of professional knowledge and attitudes. In recognition of this, probation trainees sign their court reports as 'Acting, Temporary, or Assistant Probation Officer', and students in other settings may be given such titles as 'Student Social Worker' or 'Student Child Care Officer' or simply 'Social Worker'. Giving them a different name does not alter the fact that students are students, but it sometimes gives them a greater confidence with clients, and it also proclaims the fact that the agency considers them capable of carrying responsibility.

The supervisor and the student

1. *Supervisory sessions.* Every student should be able to have a regular weekly session with his supervisor. The

importance of this cannot be over-emphasised. In addition, the student will have to discuss specific points, ask for guidance or information in relation to his cases, or be prepared by the supervisor for taking on new work: but no matter how much *ad hoc* supervision of this kind is given, it is no substitute for a regular, fixed time, when supervisor and student meet to discuss the student's work and progress. Supervisors are busy people, and in present circumstances it is unrealistic to expect that all supervisors will always be able to ensure that other demands do not encroach on the time which should belong to the student, but none the less every possible effort should be made to prevent this happening. Students who have had regular sessions with their supervisors value this enormously, and never fail to express their appreciation, while those who have had most of their supervision 'on the run' are always aware of the fact that they could have had more help, and would have learned more, if it had been possible to have a more fixed structure for supervisory teaching.

About an hour and a half is the usual time allowed for each supervisory session, and if this time can be set aside, from the beginning of the placement, at a fixed time each week, this gives the best chance of ensuring that student and supervisor meet regularly, for a period of uninterrupted discussion. The supervisor benefits from this way of working as well as the student. If the student knows that they will definitely be meeting within a few days to discuss his work, he will find it more possible to contain his anxieties and his questions until then than if he does not know when his supervisor will be available, and so feels that he had better snatch any opportunity for discussion which presents itself. Although there are bound to be occasions when a student needs to discuss a particular situation here and now, either because an immediate decision is required, or because his own anxiety is too overwhelming, it is part of training to learn to contain anxiety up to a point, and to distinguish the situations which require an immediate decision from those which may safely wait.

Where a supervisor has more than one student, or even where there are a number of students in the agency, each with a different supervisor, it is often possible to give some group teaching. Providing information about the agency, teaching related to specific procedures, and discussion of case material, can all be usefully done in a group. Students often find it particularly stimulating and interesting to discuss a case which one of them is handling, and the experience offered by group discussion provides something different from the usual individual sessions with the supervisor. Such group meetings can provide a useful addition to the student's experience, but they should not be used as a substitute for regular supervision.

2. *The relationship between supervisor and student.* (a) *Teacher and learner.* The personal relationship which is established between the individual student and his supervisor is as important as any other teaching (or casework) relationship, and must be based on the acceptance by both people involved, that one is in the role of a teacher and the other a learner. This appears an obvious statement, but will perhaps bear elaboration since supervisors and students do not always find this relationship entirely easy to accept. Students whose main experience has been in school and university are accustomed to being learners, and do not usually find the position uncomfortable (even though they may be getting tired of it). Those who come to professional training, either from other fields of employment, or after some years' experience in social work, inevitably have some adjustment to make, and do not always find it easy to return to a situation where they are once again learners.

Similarly supervisors, particularly new ones, are not always prepared to accept the role of teacher, with all that it implies. They may not be sufficiently sure of their own skills to feel competent to teach, in which case it becomes difficult to accept responsibility for what the student learns. Such supervisors probably tend to provide the student with work, and to offer some guidance and advice gleaned from their own experiences, but have only rather vague ideas about what the student has to learn, and even less definite plans about what they have to teach. Reluctance to accept that one has to teach as a supervisor, may simply be due to the fact that the supervisor concerned really wants to be left to be a social worker, and has no desire to teach her skills: it may be that she has had too little time to consolidate her own learning since she trained, or (a fairly common reason) it may be because she does not really recognise that the supervisor is an educator.

(b) *Authority*. Both students and supervisors sometimes encounter difficulties related to their own feelings about authority. This is a topic which every social worker has discussed in the course of training, and probably many times since, but it is one that cannot be avoided here. Several pages have already been devoted to a discussion of the responsibilities of a supervisor as an educator, a helper, and an administrator, and in each of these areas she must accept the authority to carry out her responsibilities. The agency delegates to her the authority to hold the student accountable for his work, and to ensure that clients are given competent service; the training course, in accepting her as a supervisor, delegates authority to teach the student, and to evaluate his progress and competence in practice. The student knows that his supervisor has this authority, whether or not it is openly acknowledged. If both of them can accept the fact, and the inevitable difference in professional status which it brings, it will leave the supervisor more free to teach, and the student to learn, than if either tries to pretend that their relationship is no different from that which exists between colleagues of equal standing.

This raises the whole question of how formal the relationship should be between a supervisor and a student. In settings which are intentionally informal, such as Family Service Units, a student will, of course, be treated as the rest of the staff, and probably first names will be used by both supervisor and student. In more formal settings it is sometimes more difficult to decide how a student should be addressed. There are so many variations between agencies as to whether first names are used among the staff; sometimes professional staff address each other by their first names, but are more formal when talking to clerical or senior staff, while in other agencies first names are seldom used within the office. However a supervisor decides that she and her student should address each other, there are two points to bear in mind. First, it should fit into the general pattern existing in the agency between senior and junior professional staff, and secondly, the formality or informality of the relationship should be decided upon because it seems to be the most helpful to the students in the agency, and not purely for the personal comfort of either supervisor or student. The use of first names and complete informality can sometimes denote a reluctance on the part of the supervisor to accept her position in relation to students, and, equally, strict formality may be a way of keeping students at a distance, and refusing to allow them to know the supervisor as a person. In establishing a relationship with each student, a supervisor has to be sensitive to the student's expectations of her, which will be influenced by his past experiences with other teachers and people in authority. He may be quite at ease and looking forward with interest to this new relationship, or he may view her warily, and prefer to keep at a distance, or sometimes he may try to neutralise what he sees as a potentially threatening situation, by trying to establish a completely informal and friendly relationship. To have more than one student in an agency may be helpful, in that students do not need to rely so heavily on agency staff for social as well as professional relationships. If several students share the same supervisor this may sometimes create a certain degree of competition for the supervisor's attention, particularly with more immature students. It can also be an experience from which they can be helped to learn something about themselves, and to prepare for employment, where they certainly will not have the individual attention of a senior member of staff.

3. *The beginning of supervision.* (a) *Orientation.* The first few days in a new placement will be a period of orientation for the student : he will be finding his way about, getting to know the agency, and probably meeting, or at least reading about, the clients with whom he is going to work. He also needs to discover quite early what his supervisor expects of him, and what responsibilities he carries in relation to his own learning, for in a teaching/learning relationship, as in any other, the responsibilities do not all rest on one side.

First, the student will want to know when his weekly supervision session has been fixed, how long he may expect it to last, and in what ways he will be asked to prepare for it. He may be expected to hand in a case record beforehand, or to suggest a particular topic which he would like to discuss, or for some sessions his supervisor may decide that he needs to think about one particular aspect of his work.

Second, he has to know what kind of records he will be expected to write, and for what purpose. For teaching purposes his supervisor may want him to write very full records, and she may wish him to record all, or only selected, visits and interviews in this way; for the agency files, quite brief records are often all that is required, and on some of his cases the student may be writing reports for the information of magistrates, psychiatrists, doctors, or other social workers.

Third, the student has to be made as secure as possible in the role of a learner, which means that he has to have 'permission' to make mistakes. No one learns if they cannot take some risks, and in learning a new skill, mistakes are inevitable. A student needs to know that it is all right if he does not do everything well, and also that his supervisor will protect him from becoming involved in situations too far beyond his competence, where his mistakes might really do harm to his clients.

(b) *Educational diagnosis*. During the first weeks of a placement, it is useful if the supervisor can produce an educational 'diagnosis' for each student, which may not actually be written down, although in effect it often takes the form of an interim evaluation. The supervisor should have had some information about the student's stage of learning before he arrives, so that she has been able to plan some experiences for him, and during his first weeks with the agency she will be able to reach a clearer 'diagnosis'. Included in it will be the student's educational needs, how these may be met in his placement, and the learning goals, short- and long-term, which student and supervisor have agreed upon. The supervisor will gather information for this 'diagnosis' from two main sources: her observation of the student and his work, and his own assessment of his educational needs which she will have discussed with him. In addition, she will have some idea of how he learns. One student will like to get as much theoretical knowledge as

44

possible 'under his belt' before going into the live situation, which he will try to fit into the theoretical framework. Another will tend to mistrust theory, and can really only learn it by fitting it, piece by piece, into his actual experience. Some students are 'plodders', learning slowly and thoroughly, others make dramatic progress with plateaux in between where they show no apparent movement. No learning is once for all time: it is not a steady upward progression, but is subject to lapses, when the learner reverts to former ways of behaving, but the two-steps-forward-one-step-back pattern does still move forward. Knowing something about the general patterns of learning, and his own particular ways of operating as a learner, is helpful to a student. He is less liable to be discouraged by setbacks if he realises that they are a normal part of learning, and his own slowness or quickness can be more easily regarded as an individual characteristic, rather than as worse, or better, than other students.

The supervisor who is prepared to discuss with her student the educational purpose of the plans she has for him, and to make him more conscious of how he learns as an individual, is helping the student to work and to learn with greater purpose. A simple example: a student who is himself quick-thinking and energetic might tend to want results quickly and so push his clients at a faster pace than they can manage. His supervisor might decide to give him some work with a family where she knows that the client finds difficulty in accepting help, and where the student must not force the pace. The student might find this frustrating, but is more likely to make a real effort to learn from the experience, if he knows his supervisor's purpose in giving him this family to work with.

Much of this chapter has been concerned with the planning and preparation which is so necessary if a supervisor is to be able to give each student the best experience which her agency can offer. Some of the arrangements for students, such as the machinery for allocating work to them, can be set up once and continue to operate for successive students, but the supervisor will find that her work with other members of the agency staff in relation to students will be continuous. Staff whose first concern is not with training can find a stream of new people irritating, and they can quickly lose any initial enthusiasm. A supervisor has to work to keep an interest in students alive, and must deal with the frictions which inevitably arise; she has to help the agency to tolerate less competent, as well as good, students. In short, the suggestions which have been made in this chapter about providing a structure for teaching and learning do not just apply to the beginning of a placement, because much of the 'structure' is in the form of human relationships, between supervisor and agency staff, as much as between supervisor and student. And human relationships require to be tended.

IV

Selecting cases for a student

The choice of work suitable for students is so often a problem for supervisors themselves, and for other agency staff who may be asked to 'lend' cases, that it seems appropriate to devote a section to this subject. The first thing which needs to be said is that each student has something to offer clients, even though he may be unaware of it himself. It is important that the supervisor should recognise this, and try from the beginning to provide opportunities for the student to make use of any special experience or interests which he may have, in work with clients. Even a very young student has within himself and his own life experience the foundations on which to build the professional skills of a social worker : he has listened and talked to other people, he has made relationships within his family and outside it, and if he stops to think, he has doubtless helped other people, and been helped himself at different times during his life. These experiences he brings with him, together with his warmth, his concern for people, and his desire to be helpful, and he has something of real value to offer, even if it does not yet approach the levels of a professional skill. Older students have longer life experience, and probably several years of employment behind them, and will have something different to give to clients; they are often more assured about meeting people, and have a wider knowledge, but they are not necessarily any more confident of their ability to help, than is a younger student.

A word of warning is necessary about students who already have experience in other fields of work. It is easy to assume, for example, that a student with nursing experience will find no difficulty in dealing with a health problem, or that an ex-policeman will be at ease in a court. In fact it is often extremely difficult for a student to find himself in a familiar setting but in a new role, and such a student will need help in sorting out the functions of a social worker as opposed to those of a nurse, or of a policeman. In a familiar situation one tends to behave in the way which one has discovered to be appropriate in the past and it is often harder to unlearn than it is to learn afresh.

Finding at the beginning of training that he has something of value to offer will help to increase the student's self-confidence, and enable him to build on such knowledge and experience as he already possesses. The supervisor should try to ensure that cases selected for his learning are also likely to provide the student with this most necessary reassurance. Ideally one plans to start a beginning student on easy tasks and gradually give him work requiring greater skill and knowledge as his competence increases: in reality, this ordered progression often proves impracticable. Simple cases may quickly become complicated ones, and what is easy for one student may, for personal reasons, be quite difficult for another. Supervisors are often more worried than students about the impossibility of ensuring that any work given to a student will remain easy and simple. They get anxious about students' being too upset, about the client, and also, quite naturally, about their own responsibility in the matter, including what may be said in the agency if a student fails to manage the situation. The advantages and disadvantages of allowing a student to keep a complicated case are discussed later, but the supervisor's anxieties are mentioned here because they are a factor which affects the type of cases selected for a student. The more confident a supervisor, the less she is controlled by her own anxieties, and the more able to select work in terms of the student's educational needs and his capabilities, rather than in terms of her own limitations as a supervisor.

Sharing work with a student

If a student is without previous field work experience, or has only a short placement, it may not be appropriate to give him complete responsibility for work with a client or family, but he does need to be given a chance to do, as well as to observe. Students hate feeling useless, and will usually welcome being given a task even if it is limited. They should not just be used to run errands for the rest of the staff, but sometimes they can give help with specific tasks, or take over part of the work on a case which the supervisor or another social worker is carrying. The student's time is not being wasted even if he is given quite mundane jobs to do, provided that his supervisor takes the time to help him to learn something from them.

At this early stage of training, a student needs opportunities to observe and to listen. He also has to begin to try himself out in contact with clients as a representative of the agency, to learn how the social services fit together, and what specific functions each fulfils. The student who accompanies his supervisor on visits needs to be given sufficient information about the client or family to enable him to listen and observe intelligently. He should also be clear about whether he is expected to play any part in the interview, and if he has the responsibility for writing it up afterwards.

Quite soon, the student may begin to undertake visits on his own, often as an 'assistant' to the social worker. There may be information to be conveyed to, or obtained from, a client, and in certain settings where clients may be receiving regular visits as a supportive measure, the student may undertake these for the period of time he is with the agency. There may also be opportunities for a student to give some special attention to a particular member of a family, who would be likely to benefit from a more exclusive relationship than the family's worker can usually offer.

Such activities give a student some independence, definite tasks, and provide experiences which he can be asked to record for his supervisor. He will discover how observant he is, how well he listens, and in discussion he may be able to put forward his ideas and opinions about the people he has met, and what causes their problems.

Dividing work with clients between a social worker and a student can present some problems in relation to where responsibilities rest. In a shared case, the social worker concerned (whether she be the student's supervisor or not) has to decide, and make clear to the student, and probably to the clients also, whether the student is acting on her behalf and undertaking jobs which she would normally do herself, or whether he has a specific piece of work to do with the client or a member of his family, for which he will take responsibility under the guidance of the social worker to whom the case belongs. One student may be apprehensive of accepting responsibility and happy to remain in the role of an assistant social worker, while another may be eager to assume a greater professional independence than his competence and experience warrant. Any student, whatever his attitude, needs to understand clearly the degree of responsibility assigned to him in a case which he shares with the social worker. He is freer to use his initiative appropriately, even if it is within fairly narrow limits, if he understands what is expected of him in the situation.

To share a case with a supervisor, in the sense of being present at interviews, or accompanying the supervisor on visits to a client's home, can be useful for a beginning student in letting him observe how a social worker goes about his job. It can also give him confidence in approaching his own interviews, if it helps him to realise that the way a social worker talks with a client is not something utterly different and unrelated to any ordinary discussion between two people. However, there may also be disadvantages of which supervisors should be aware.

A student who is able to perceive the skill involved in conducting a good interview can be discouraged and feel that he can never achieve such competence, or alternatively he may feel that he should try to model himself on his supervisor. Neither attitude is going to help the student to develop his own skills.

Allocating cases to a student

Once a student has reached the stage of professional training, if not before, he has to take full responsibility under supervision for work with a limited number of cases. This means that the student not only undertakes all contacts with the client, in interviews or visits, on the telephone and by letter, but he will also be responsible for discussing the case with other colleagues or agencies, keeping the case record up to date, and preparing and presenting any necessary reports to case conferences, committees or courts. If at the very beginning of training a student is felt to have insufficient experience to undertake all aspects of the work on a particular case, the supervisor may have to give some help, but long before the end of training the student should be carrying his own cases fully, undertaking the same tasks as an employed member of the agency's staff as far as possible, and being given responsibility for his work. His supervisor will, of course, assume some responsibility for the student's work, and must be aware of what he is doing, and the standard he is able to achieve, but the student must carry his workload himself.

Common anxieties

1. *The student's inexperience*. Supervisors (and sometimes students too) may be somewhat concerned about giving students this degree of responsibility, for a number of reasons. One of the most common anxieties among students and new supervisors is that the student's inexperience will be the cause of his making mistakes which will be harmful to his clients. If the supervisor is discussing the student's work with him in some detail, and is helping him to think ahead, and to anticipate possible events intelligently, the most likely mistake that the student will make is one of omission – failing to take up what a client says to him, or missing an opportunity. Sometimes a student tries to force a faster pace than the client is ready to accept, or he thrusts his new-found knowledge about human behaviour at someone who is neither willing nor able to understand it. Inexperienced students can be unwittingly clumsy in handling their relationships with clients too, but it is the rare client who is so vulnerable and sensitive that a mistake resulting from the student's inexperience is going to cause any lasting harm to him. Fortunately,

clients have their defences, and most supervisors with experience would probably agree that the good will of the student and his genuine desire to be of help, go some way to protecting both him and his client from any real hurt arising from the student's inexperience.

2. *The client's reaction.* All of us enjoy feeling indispensable from time to time, and this perhaps has something to do with the implied anxiety sometimes expressed that a client will suffer if his worker changes for a period of time. Continuity is important, of course, and there are certain clients who might be deeply upset at a temporary change of worker, but there are many more who are able to accept, and often to use constructively, the help of a different worker, provided that they are not being asked to accept a succession of changes. Clients may miss their accustomed social worker if they have a student working with them, and sometimes the change seems to result in an exacerbation of symptoms, or problems and difficulties being more clearly shown. This is not necessarily a disaster, and on occasion can even result in the student being able to help the client to come to grips with some aspect of his problem which he has not really been able to face before.

3. *The supervisor's uncertainties.* How does the supervisor know just what the student is really doing with the client if there is no one else present at his interviews, and maybe no other worker sees the client, until after the student has left the agency? This anxiety sometimes results in a new supervisor feeling that she must have occasional contact with the student's clients, or at least they must all be 'safe' clients whom she knows well herself. She can thus assess whether the student's judgement is sound, and whether he seems to be handling the client well. The requirement that the student's records are as full as possible, and include the student's own part in interviews, in fact

make it possible to have a reasonably clear idea of how a student is handling a particular situation. The supervisor also gets to know the student as a person, and is able to observe his reactions, and the relationships he makes with other staff in the agency, all of which will provide additional clues to the way he is likely to be relating to his clients. The student who is relaxed, friendly and warm in his contacts within the agency is not likely to be a completely different person when he is with a client; equally a shy, tense student is probably much the same with clients – though he may of course be more at ease with them than with colleagues!

The necessary contacts between the student and other members of staff may be another source of anxiety to supervisors who are being asked to entrust the full conduct of a case to the student. For example, a supervisor may understandably feel that a student in a hospital should not be put in the position of having to work with a ward sister or a consultant who is impatient with social work and intolerant of students, so that she must either undertake contacts of this kind herself or avoid giving the student patients on certain wards. In addition, it may be vital to preserve a hard-won working relationship between the medical social worker and another member of the hospital staff, and the supervisor may decide that she cannot risk straining it by introducing a student. Both supervisor and student quite legitimately require protection to some extent, and if a student's confidence is going to be demolished, or co-operation between members of the hospital staff endangered by arranging for the student to work in certain situations, then obviously it is better to avoid predictable trouble. However, students will soon be social workers and few social workers are employed in an administrative setting which is always congenial, or are entirely surrounded by colleagues with whom they see eye to eye. It is better to have experienced the reality of the setting while a student than to come up against it for the first time in employment. This holds true in any field of social work, and the point has been clearly illustrated in a recently published study of the work experience of a group of newly qualified medical social workers.[1]

4. *Difficult cases.* When a student's case turns out to be more difficult than anticipated, should it be taken back from the student, or should he be allowed to continue to work with it? It must be said at the outset that in some situations the student does have to be relieved of a responsibility which he cannot manage, for the client's or the agency's sake, as well as his own. However, a decision to transfer a case to a more experienced worker always needs careful consideration. Once a student has got to know a client, he does not usually want to lose the case, even if it is difficult, and if the case does have to be transferred the student's own feelings about this need to be recognised. He may be happy to be relieved of a difficult situation, but he is also likely to feel he has let his client down, and his own self-confidence is unlikely to be increased, however realistic the reasons for transfer. If it is at all possible, it is usually better to try to help the student to carry the case himself, and, given real help and support, even quite inexperienced students sometimes surprise their supervisors and themselves by the standard of work they are able to achieve. If a student is able to meet the challenge of a difficult piece of work, he not only learns from it, he also proves to himself that he can survive the strain of a worrying and demanding case, and above all, that he can do a job as a social worker.

Transferring cases to a student

The supervisor has an important task in seeing that there is adequate preparation for transferring cases to a student. If done carefully, this minimises the risk of difficulties for the client and the student, and for other social workers in the agency, whose cases may be temporarily transferred to a student's caseload. Clients need to understand as clearly as possible what the situation is: i.e. that for a period of time they will be having a new worker who will assume full responsibility for working with them, in the same way that their usual worker does. During this time they will have no direct contact with their accustomed worker, but she will be hearing how they are faring, and keeping up with news of them.

Opinions differ as to the advisability of telling clients from the beginning how long the student will be with the agency and it is sometimes suggested that it is better to leave it to the student to prepare them for his departure a few weeks before the end of the placement. Either way, there are advantages and disadvantages, and the course of action must be decided according to the needs of each client. The important point is that the client should understand quite clearly that the worker who is taking over his case is taking it over completely, and that this arrangement is being made with the approval and co-operation of the usual worker. To prepare a client by saying, 'You are going to have a student for the next six months', or half promising to drop in sometime and see how things are going, is not calculated to make a client feel any confidence in the student, nor can it raise the client's self-esteem to feel perhaps that his affairs are so unimportant that they can be handed over to a student to deal with.

It is not suggested that student supervisors themselves

would be unaware of the sensitivity needed to prepare a client for transfer to a student, but not all other workers in agencies are sympathetic to the needs of training, and some very much dislike the idea of handing over their clients for a student to learn on. The supervisor, or whoever is responsible for the whole training programme of the agency, often needs to discuss with other workers how they will prepare their clients for transfer, and how they will introduce the student.

Keeping other workers in the picture

In connection with other staff in the agency, the supervisor also has a responsibility for making arrangements to keep the usual worker informed about what is happening with her clients while they are on the student's caseload. This can usually be done most easily by arranging for the worker to see the student's records of his visits or interviews before they are finally filed on the casepaper. In addition, the worker to whom the case belongs has a right to the assurance that no significant decisions will be taken without prior consultation. Such arrangements within the agency take time, but it is well spent if it helps to produce a positive attitude to training, and reduces the risk of clients and students alike suffering as a result of staff conflicts and tensions.

The student's caseload

A supervisor has to keep in view a composite picture of the student's total work load, as well as considering carefully each individual case to be given to a student, in order to ensure that he has the right quantity of work, and the kind of cases which are appropriate for his learning needs.

1. *Quantity.* In terms of quantity, the student needs enough to keep him well occupied during the period of

time he is in the agency, but not so much to do that he has insufficient time to study his cases carefully. It may be argued that it is unrealistic to allow a student to carry only a very small caseload, so that he has a good deal of time to spend on each case, as this will not prepare him for the pressure of work which he will have to face as soon as he enters employment, particularly if he is working in the statutory services. Yet if advantage is not taken of the opportunity to be a student and to take time to study, there may never be another chance to learn to do the job properly. Those concerned with training are aware of the current conditions in which social workers are employed, and they try to prepare students realistically for the job they will be doing, but this does not absolve them of the responsibility of teaching the principles of good social work practice, nor of insisting that students acquire professional skills of a sufficiently high standard. The only way to learn how to do anything well is by practice and analysis. If one attempts to learn by practice only, without time for analysing what one is doing and why, faults may go uncorrected and the activity is more likely to be mechanical than purposeful.

A student's total work load must, therefore, allow for an amount of time for writing records and studying cases which would be disproportionate to the work load of an employed member of staff. It is not easy to suggest a suitable number of cases for a student to carry, as it must depend upon the amount of work to be done on each case, the student's stage of learning, and the demands which the particular cases are likely to make upon him. For example, a family with many problems, perhaps requiring very frequent visiting, may also involve a student in discussions with workers in other agencies, case conferences etc., and he will have to record all that he does. One or two families of this type may occupy a student exclusively for a period of time, and occupy not only his time, but also his thinking, and his full capacity for learning. It is easy to forget that learning itself takes up energy, quite apart from that expended in carrying out the actual job, and students are under the pressure of learning, even if they are not under pressure of work.

2. *Types of case.* There is no such thing as a 'model' caseload for a student, but in selecting cases, the supervisor can keep in mind certain general questions which may help her to decide whether she is choosing the kind of work which is likely to be helpful to the learning of this particular student. Taking into consideration the student's stage in training, the length of the placement, and the situation of the clients themselves, what may he be able to learn from working with this group of cases? Is he likely to be able to see that he has achieved something? What realistic hope is there that any of the cases will show movement before the student leaves the agency? Perhaps all the cases need not give the student a sense of achievement, nor all show much movement, but within the total caseload there should be a sufficient chance for him to achieve a degree of success in some areas, and to be able to see some change, no matter how slight, in the client's attitude to, and way of dealing with, his problem. An example may serve to illustrate the point.

A student moving into a Child Guidance Clinic as the second placement of a professional course was given a caseload which included two cases, an adolescent girl, and a small boy whose father had died some time before. The girl was already known to the clinic, but the little boy was a new patient. The student herself had some experience with adolescent girls, and enjoyed working with them, and she wanted experience of working directly with younger children.

The supervisor selected these two cases with the student's needs in mind. Work with an adolescent girl was something about which the student would feel confident, and in which she was likely to be quite successful. The little boy's difficulties seemed to arise mainly from his distress at his father's death, which the rest of the family could not allow him to express, so that it seemed likely that he could be helped immediately to some extent, by being able to talk about how he felt. This case provided the student with the opportunity to work directly with a child, and the possibility of seeing some movement in the boy's ability to deal with his feelings about the loss of his father. There were, of course, other aspects to these cases, which have here been oversimplified, and the student also worked with other clients, but the two cases illustrate how a supervisor can try to plan a caseload to meet a student's educational needs.

Many supervisors like to build up a student's caseload from new work coming to the agency, and there is much to recommend this plan. At the beginning of any contact between a social work agency and a client there is always a certain amount to be accomplished. The student will have to obtain information about the client and his difficulties, and share in the decision about whether he has come to the appropriate agency. He will have to explain the function of the agency to the client, and what will be expected of him in his continued contact with the service: he must use his diagnostic skills, to try to make some assessment of the situation. Events often move quickly at the beginning of a case, particularly if the client has arrived at the agency at a point of crisis, and a student can both learn a great deal and be of help to the client, even if he is not in the agency long enough to see the case right through to the end.

Supervisors should on the whole avoid giving the type of case where the outcome is inevitable, unless they really feel that the particular student needs this experience. For example, students who are going to be in an agency for only a few months should not be asked to take on families or individual clients, whom numerous other social workers have attempted to help, with no apparent success. It is very unlikely that an inexperienced student is going to be able to succeed in a short time, where experienced workers have been unable to accomplish anything over a number of years, and it is unfair to the student to put him in a situation where he must fail. Students have to come to terms with the inescapable realities which all of us find hard to face, but too many cases where it seems to the student that there can be no satisfactory outcome, are discouraging. Not everybody recovers when they are ill, mental or physical handicaps often have to be lived with, and ageing is an inevitable process; some people have been so damaged by their life experiences that they have little or no capacity to use help. Yet too much experience of this kind of reality, all at once, can severely hinder a student's learning. It also has to be remembered that with a small caseload, it is difficult for a student to keep a sense of proportion about his difficulties. He may be carrying a total of five or six cases, and if, for example, two of them are going through a difficult phase, and only one of the others seems to be moving, the overall picture may look very gloomy. Students may sometimes need help in recognising that the process of learning on a small number of cases does inevitably magnify problems, and that the social worker who is carrying a full caseload does not normally experience such a large proportion of his cases 'going wrong' at the same time.

The emphasis which has been placed on the educational needs of the student throughout this chapter may seem unrealistic to some supervisors, who, if they have a constant stream of students coming, must sometimes feel that the student is lucky to get a caseload at all, never mind trying to select cases which will suit his particular needs. The agency's primary function is to serve clients, not to educate students, and those whose first concern is training rather than practice, have to remember that a student's caseload has to be drawn from the ordinary work of the agency, and clients cannot be produced to order. At the same time, an awareness of the educational needs of the particular student acts as a general guide to the supervisor in selecting his cases, and if it is impossible to provide work at the beginning of the placement which meets all his needs, it often happens that other more suitable cases become available during the placement.

REFERENCE

(1) *The First Two Years*, Institute of Medical Social Workers, 1965, pp. 51 ff.

V

Case records

The student's case records occupy a position of central importance in his learning in field work, and he should be encouraged to regard record keeping as an integral part of casework not just a tiresome chore. Under the general heading of case records, this chapter includes a discussion of other written documents, such as social histories, court reports and letters.

Purposes for which case records are kept

1. From the viewpoint of the agency, case records have to be kept as a record of the work undertaken by the agency. Moreover, in certain statutory services there are official rules governing the kind of reports which must be written, how frequently they must be produced, and even what they should include. The keeping of records is a method that an agency uses to demonstrate that it is carrying out its functions. In certain services the records are open to official inspection, and may be used to provide statistical data about the amount and kind of work an agency has undertaken in any given period. In addition, the keeping of accurate records is an essential safeguard to

both agency staff and clients in situations where the agency's responsibilities, and the procedures to be used, are spelt out in legislation. For example, an N.S.P.C.C. Inspector or Child Care Officer who is responsible for investigations of neglect or cruelty to children, must keep exact and careful records of his work to protect both himself and the agency, and even more important, to ensure that his observations and actions are on record to be used, if necessary, to take legal action to protect the child, or to protect his parents against unfounded allegations of neglect or cruelty.

2. Case records are or should be part of casework, to be used by the worker to clarify thinking, to help him keep track not only of events, but also of movement in the case, and finally to help him evaluate his own work. Case records, therefore, should contain diagnostic and evaluative material as well as narrative. They are used by the caseworker himself, but also by other workers who may be concerned with the case, either temporarily because of the usual worker's absence, or because the case has to be transferred for administrative reasons.

Types of recording

1. *Verbatim.* This is the type of recording which sets out the dialogue exactly, or almost exactly, as it was spoken, as in a theatrical script. It is not normally used in case records, but beginning students sometimes seem to find it the easiest way to recall an interview, or part of it. It also has the advantage of reducing the possibility of the student's attempting to select or re-arrange material before he is competent to do so. Individuals vary in the extent to which they can recall even parts of an interview verbatim, and for some students the very prospect of having to do so might inhibit spontaneity in the interview itself.

At a very early stage of training, a student may be encouraged to record his observations, as well as the conversation. A social worker has to be observant to a high degree, able to register in his mind the material details of a home he visits, and the physical characteristics of the person he is interviewing. Moreover, he has to be able to record his observations with accuracy. Students themselves are sometimes concerned about evaluating physical conditions, because they have no standards for judging, except personal ones, and recording observations accurately at an early stage of training can help a student to start considering physical standards, as well as increasing his powers of observation. People under stress often show more of their feelings than they are able to express verbally, and one way of helping a student to observe and to interpret what a client is 'saying' with his actions, or by the signs of stress which he cannot control, is by encouraging him to put his observations on paper.

2. *Process recording*. There is much confusion about this type of recording, what it is, when and why it should be used. Process recording should do what it says: describe in chronological sequence the *process* of an interview, or of group interaction. It is designed to highlight interpersonal relations, and it therefore has to be a very detailed record, including the worker's contribution as much as that of the client or group. Gordon Hamilton[1] uses the analogy of a slow motion picture to describe process recording, a written record which enables the reader to 'watch' the details of action and interaction in personal relationships. The following example of process recording is taken from an interview with a mother, who is telling the social worker about one of her little girls who had been placed with foster parents and subsequently adopted by them.

Hilary had gone to live with a foster mother, and had got on wonderfully well, so that eventually the foster mother had asked to adopt her. To help Mrs. Hammond make up her mind about releasing Hilary for adoption, the Child Care Officer had taken her to see Hilary, and Mrs. Hammond could hardly believe how she had changed. Mrs. Hammond said of course Hilary had not known her, and had said, 'Hullo, lady.' As she told me, Mrs. Hammond's eyes filled with tears, and she said she would never forget the moment. Her own child greeting her like that! Mrs. Hammond said she took ages to decide to let Hilary be adopted, although she had met the foster mother and thought her a very nice person. She pointed out Hilary's picture still hanging on the wall, as she told me that she still thought about Hilary and often wondered how she was.

I said that it must have been very hard to let Hilary go, and I was sure that Mrs. Hammond would never forget her. Mrs. Hammond said that it had seemed best for Hilary, for she would not have felt it right to take her away from what she was used to. I replied that it sometimes took more love to let a child go because it seemed the right thing to do, than to keep her.

The purpose served by this recording is to show in some detail how Mrs. Hammond expressed her continued conflict about having allowed her daughter to be adopted, and the way in which the social worker responded by acknowledging how hard the decision must have been, and also showing that she understood that Mrs. Hammond had not just rejected Hilary, but had been, and still was, concerned for the child. The record shows how the two people in the situation responded to each other and, within the brief extract given, one has a glimpse of the acceptance and support which the social worker is trying to offer in her relationship with Mrs. Hammond.

Students are asked to write process records as an aid to learning the skills of a professional social worker. No record can be completely accurate, and the student's ability to recall what took place in a particular interview will be influenced by a number of factors, not least, it is sometimes suggested, by an unwillingness to remember parts of an interview which were difficult for him. Selection of material recalled is bound to be subjective to some extent, but a record is not useless for teaching purposes simply because it is an abridged version of the original event. Students quickly come to value what they learn from process recording, and are better able to record with full honesty as they discover how constructively such records can be used.

A social worker who has learned the value of process recording does not necessarily abandon it entirely when he finishes training; he may use it to highlight a particular part of an interview, which he wants to stress in the record, or he may find that a specially puzzling or difficult interview may be at least partly clarified by writing a process record of it.

3. *Condensed recording.* Few agencies require, or even permit, social workers to produce process records of their day-to-day work for the files, and indeed such records are of necessity so long that they would be impractical to keep, and impossible to read for all ordinary purposes. A shorter, more condensed form of recording is therefore used in most agencies, which is either narrative or topical in style, or a mixture of the two. For both the worker has to select the material to be recorded, keeping it mainly in chronological order if he is writing in the narrative style, or rearranging it under different topics, if he decides that this style of recording is more appropriate. Students must

write full and detailed records, but in the course of training they must also learn to produce more concise records which are appropriate for agency files. Learning to write shorter records involves learning to select what material to record as significant, what to discard as unimportant or merely repetitious, and this is something which many students find difficult. The selection of material for recording requires clear thinking, and the acceptance of a professional responsibility to decide what is important, and why it is. Throughout training, students are adding to their knowledge and understanding of human behaviour. As the possible significance of events, comments, and reactions becomes more apparent to them, so they perceive more clearly the complexity of human affairs, and the many contributing factors from the past and the present which have their influence in shaping the situation with which the client and the student are now attempting to deal. This wider and deeper perspective, together with the knowledge that someone else is probably going to have to work with the client after he has left the agency, sometimes makes a student feel that he must try and record 'all he knows', because he feels incompetent to select what is really important now, or may prove to be important in the future. This is an area in which supervisors often need to give some help, not merely suggesting to a student that he condense a process record for the file, but holding him to thinking carefully about what to retain and what to discard, and the reasons for doing so.

4. *Summarised recording.* This type of recording is often used at a specific stage in the casework, and usually in addition to the ordinary condensed recording. Summarised recording is used in a casework review, when events over the past months are summarised briefly, and an assessment of progress made. Short but complete pieces of work, such

as a study of a prospective foster home, an application for service, or a court enquiry, may be recorded in a summary which represents a number of interviews or visits.

Statutory agencies usually have official rulings about the way records are to be kept; most often they are of the diary type, where the social worker is required to record each interview or visit, so in practice summarised recording is most frequently used for some kind of assessment, of which some specific examples have already been suggested. In requiring students to write summaries, whether in closing or transferring a case, or in, for example, a foster home study, supervisors have to see to it that the student really does take some responsibility for setting out his assessment of the situation. A social worker has a responsibility to record the events and the facts in any piece of work he undertakes, but he should not then leave it to the reader to assess the situation for himself: he should be prepared to commit to paper his professional opinion, not leaving it as a mere opinion, but supporting it with such facts as he knows, and his interpretation of them. Writing such an assessment requires clarity of thought and expression, thinking about the case, as well as knowing about it, and students may not find it easy to be asked to set out their diagnostic thinking. They are afraid they may be wrong, that they could be prejudging the issue, or misjudging the client, that their opinions may be unduly influenced by their own prejudices. None the less, assessments do have to be made, and an evaluation of the client and his situation, whether explicit or not, cannot be avoided if any action is to be taken at all; students are likely to be better social workers if they have been trained not only to think carefully about their work, but also to set down on paper the conclusions they reach, no matter how tentative they may be. A professional assessment is not intended to be for all time, it is a guide for further action, and it may be revised quite radically in the light of subsequent events.

Other written documents

In addition to being able to keep social work records, students have to learn to produce reports and letters which will be sent out of the agency. These may go out over the signature of individual social workers, or they may be signed by the head of the agency, but whichever is the case, the responsibility for the letter or report must rest with the writer. Social workers write to people of all kinds, not only to their clients or to other social workers, and they have to learn to phrase their letters and reports in ways which are comprehensible and acceptable to the recipients. Sometimes students have difficulty in writing certain letters, for example, to officials or colleagues in other disciplines, and may need some assistance with this. To help a student to think clearly about the purpose of the report or letter which he has to write, and the possible reactions of the person who will read it, may help to suggest that he thinks along the lines suggested by the following questions: Is the letter (or report) intended to convey information only, or does it convey a request for co-operation or action? Who is going to read it, and what might he need to know? Is the reader likely to be another social worker? If not, is the letter going to be clearly understood, or is it written in a manner which assumes an understanding of social work practice? Is the recipient likely to look on the situation in the light of a different discipline, e.g. law, medicine, education?

An appreciable amount of a social worker's job has to be done through letters and written reports, and it is all too easy to create misunderstanding, confusion or ill will by a failure to communicate clearly, with the recognition that other disciplines and agencies may have different requirements and points of view. Of particular importance are letters of referral, either requesting another agency to take over a case, or asking for an interview to be done on behalf of the writer: the exact request needs to be clearly stated, necessary background information provided, and statements about a client's attitude or behaviour without any further elaboration should be avoided. Assessments or opinions given in letters need to be supported by facts, just as a professional opinion in a case record requires the evidence for it to be stated.

Style

A social work record is a professional document, and the same standard should apply as in any other piece of writing. It should be clearly expressed, and attention should be paid to paragraphing and punctuation, which help to make it easily readable. It is possible to make a record alive and interesting without resorting to 'journalese', and students who enjoy writing sometimes need to be reminded of the professional purposes of recording. It is not of first importance that records should be entertaining to the reader, or strongly individualistic in style.

The style of letters is even more important, and students have to be able to use a variety of styles, ranging from the strictly formal to the easy, colloquial style appropriate in a letter addressed to a child. In writing to clients, students need to remember that the appearance of the letter may be important, and that in some situations it is better to send a handwritten note, or at least to use a plain envelope.

If the letter is to be opened only by the person to whom

it is addressed, it should be marked 'personal', and letters which contain confidential material should be so marked, both on the envelope and on the letter itself. References should always be quoted; and in official letters the name of the client, with identifying data such as date of birth and address, or the subject of the letter, set out at the beginning. Social workers who themselves work in small agencies do not always realise the irritation and waste of time which they can cause in a large organisation by failing to identify clearly for whom letters are intended, and what they are about. These 'secretarial' aspects of a social worker's job may seem unimportant, and something which is the concern of the agency's clerical staff, but students who are learning to use the help of typists and clerks in carrying out their tasks as social workers, should themselves know how different kinds of letters and documents should be presented.

Learning from records

Students' own case records, and those written by other workers, are constantly used in teaching. The same record may teach students different things, according to the stage of learning which each has reached, but a supervisor should have some idea of what she hopes the student will learn from any record he may be studying. He will often learn other things too, but if the educational purpose of the supervisor's job is to be taken seriously, the student's learning cannot be left entirely to chance and his own capacity to select what he needs from the material.

1. *Other workers' records.* Students are given other workers' record to study for one of two reasons: either to prepare them for meeting and working with the clients concerned, or because it is thought that the actual reading of

the case record will have some value for them, even if it is a closed case, or at any rate one with which the student will never be involved directly.

(a) Taking the second reason first, students at the beginning of training, or those who have brief observational placements, are usually given a certain number of records to read, with the purpose of introducing them to the kind of work undertaken by the agency and to the methods social workers use to serve their clients. Provided the records are reasonably well kept, and not impossibly long, the exercise can be a useful and interesting one for the student, but he will often add much more to his learning if the supervisor also has in mind some specific learning points for him, and if she shares these with him when she gives him the records he is to read.

Take for example a probation trainee, who has already had some years of employment in another field, and who is given a fairly short introductory placement in the probation service at the beginning of his training. He might be given a selection of case records to read, illustrating, for instance, work with a young man recently released from Borstal, with an older married man on probation, and with a couple referred for marital counselling, to take but three aspects of a probation officer's job. He might be asked to consider two questions: In what ways does the probation officer's task seem to differ in the three cases? If you had been asked to help these clients, to what extent do you think the knowledge you have already gained about how to work with people would have been useful? Instead of being given questions such as these, the student could have been asked to consider particularly what seemed to be the cause of each client's difficulties and to be prepared to discuss this later with the supervisor.

The aspect of the case to which the student's attention is

directed will be determined by his previous experience, practical and theoretical, and the educational aims of the particular placement. This is not to suggest that the student himself should not be consulted about which aspects of a case record interest him most, but the supervisor will probably need to help him delineate areas for special study from the mass of material, psychological, sociological and administrative, which is woven into most case records.

(b) The second reason for studying another worker's record is to prepare the student for taking over the work with the client or family. Usually he will discuss the case with his supervisor before he actually sees the client, and again this discussion may be more fruitful, particularly for a student with little experience, if he has some guidance to help him as he reads the record.

One of the most important things which a student social worker has to learn is to distinguish between evidence and speculation or opinion in a record, whether it be his own or another worker's. Both have their place, as has already been stated earlier in this chapter, but in preparing to take on a case, the student will often need help in deciding what he can really assume that he *knows* about his new client, and what must be regarded as speculation.

He will also need to begin to think about possible goals in his casework in relation to the previous worker's diagnostic thinking, or, if this is not clear, he may have to get to know the situation at first hand before he can begin to decide in what way he may be able to give help.

Before allocating the case to the student, the supervisor will already have decided that it seems to be one which this student should be able to handle, but she may find it helpful in preparing the student if she has considered two specific questions:

(i) What does the student need to know to tackle this

case? It has already been pointed out that the theoretical parts of the course cannot always keep pace with the needs of the students in their field work, and there may be aspects of the case which will be new in the student's experience. The supervisor may have to see, for example, that the student has some idea of the general problems of ageing before she gives him an elderly client to work with: in certain situations he may need some special medical or legal information. In order to be able to judge realistically where he can give help, and of what kind, the student has also to be as clear as possible about the relevant policies of the agency, and about the functions and policies of other services which may be concerned with the same client or family.

(ii) Is this student likely to have any personal reaction to this situation?

This question is perhaps particularly important to bear in mind with an inexperienced, (not necessarily young) student who may have fairly strong feelings about situations, either which reflect his own unhappy experience, or in which a client's behaviour is contrary to his own standards. The student's personal reaction to the situations he encounters has already been discussed in relation to the supervisor's responsibilities (Chapter II), and the point is raised again here in order to suggest that it can sometimes help the student in his approach to a new client if his personal reactions to the case have been discussed with him in advance. Violent quarrelling, cohabitation, drunkenness, mixed marriages, promiscuous behaviour – such things may disturb or distress him, and if he is to help a client who manifests behaviour which he personally disapproves of or cannot understand, the student will have to be given an opportunity to talk about his own feelings before he even meets the client.

It may be that the student already has the theoretical knowledge he requires, and the client's situation does not personally disturb him in any way, in which case the supervisor can go straight on to discuss how the case could be handled, if necessary helping the student to think through how to start with a client who is having a change of worker, and discussing what facts, impressions and ideas the student has gleaned from his reading of the record. As a student progresses towards the end of his training, he should normally be able to start on a case which is new to him without help, and only if the situation is specially difficult, or he himself wants to discuss it, should the supervisor need to be involved before he meets the client.

2. *The student's own records.* Students learn some of the same things from their own records as they learn from other people's, and because the two are considered separately here, it should not be taken to imply that there is a rigid division between what each can offer for the student's learning. There are, however, certain things which can only be learned from one's own records. In any case, learning through personal experience is generally more meaningful than learning from someone else's work.

The actual writing of a case record provides in itself a means of learning; it requires the student to recall and set down on paper what happened in an interview or visit, and as he goes over it in his mind, he will often become aware of aspects which he had not consciously noted at the time. It holds him to organising his thinking sufficiently to write it down so that it is intelligible to the reader, and it obliges him to select what he considers relevant material and to discard irrelevances.

If a student's record is to be used for teaching purposes, it should be put on paper *before* he discusses the visit or interview. Most supervisors have known the student who can never wait to talk about his latest experience, and there may be occasions when he should not have to wait to do this. But if the record of the interview is to be used as the basis of a supervisory session, the student must write the record before he modifies or reinterprets his ideas and impressions in the light of someone else's experience and opinion.

His own records are so closely involved with his actual experience, that they are likely to provide the student with a better opportunity for total learning, as opposed to intellectual learning, than the records of other workers can offer. Both provide material for the study of the client, his problem, and the environment in which he is living, and from both some assessment can be made of whether and how the client was helped, but only in his own records can a student study how he himself performs as a social worker. The improvement of skill must come from analysing one's own work, not another's.

REFERENCE

(1) HAMILTON, G. *Principles of Social Case Recording*, Columbia University Press, 1946, Chapter V, p. 37.

VI

Teaching from a student's records

The previous chapter ended with a brief consideration of what the student must learn from his own records, and we must now consider how the supervisor can plan her teaching. Before discussing some specific topics in detail, there are one or two general points to be made.

The greatest temptation to most teachers, and especially to new ones, is to instruct. With a new and inexperienced student, the supervisor has a wealth of information, experience and technical 'know how' to impart; she can tell, explain, correct, advise, and teach, but she has to beware that she does not do so without reference to the student's learning needs. It is easy to recognise in theory that the student's needs must guide the supervisor's teaching; it is less easy to carry it out in practice.

The supervisor's position and greater experience will often mean that she grasps, for example, what is hindering the relationship between a student and his client, while he is still unaware of it or perhaps puzzled by behaviour or reactions which he does not understand. The immediate temptation is for the supervisor to explain to the student what she thinks is happening, or to suggest how else he might go about tackling the situation. This may eventually be necessary if the student is completely baffled, but if he can be helped to find the answers instead of being given them, he is more likely to be actively learning, as opposed to being passively taught. He will need the supervisor to ask him the right questions, to focus his attention in a particular direction, perhaps to supply a piece of information which will help him to see the situation more clearly, and thus discover for himself the probable cause of the client's behaviour which is puzzling him. The understanding he achieves in this way is more likely to be absorbed than is the understanding which is given from a supervisor's wider experience. Of course it is possible to go too far in the direction of leaving the student to do the work in a supervisory session. The supervisor who never gives an answer, who always throws back the student's comments and questions, and who seems (to the student) to avoid contributing anything positive to the discussion, is not necessarily helping the student to learn in the best way possible.

Successful supervisory teaching is a question of finding a balance between offering the student sufficient stimulation in the form of knowledge and ideas, criticism and challenge, while at the same time allowing, and indeed expecting, him to learn for himself. The student who is made to think for himself, *from the very beginning* of training, is acquiring a disciplined approach to his work, which will not only help him to continue to learn in employment, but which can provide him with a support and confidence in his own ability to take hold of, and think through, the problems he will meet as a social worker.

A student in field work learns in relation to specific cases, but his learning must be transferable; that is, he must be able to extract from each case the general points which may be applicable in any similar situation, as well as understanding the uniqueness of the particular client and the set of circumstances which surround him.

For example: a student was working with a woman who had been referred by her general practitioner to a psychiatric out-patient clinic. She had several young children, and her husband had recently become totally blind. The student had to get to know this woman as a person, with her own characteristic ways of dealing with stress, to try to understand what this disaster meant to her, and to see how to help and support her, as she tried to adapt to it. From this case the student could gain knowledge and understanding which she could apply in other situations she might meet. For instance, she had in this case an illustration of the stress caused within a family by circumstances which result in an unavoidable re-allocation of roles. The wife was having to assume certain responsibilities which her husband could no longer carry while he was having to accept an enforced helplessness and dependence, with its attendant threat to his masculinity. In work with other families, the student would probably meet similar situations involving some change of roles between husband and wife.

The case could also be used to illustrate for the student that the 'sick' member of the family is often not the only one who needs help. As this wife of a newly disabled man needed to have her worry, her resentment, and her fears recognised, so, for instance, do the parents of a young delinquent, or the family of a psychiatric patient, often require their personal feelings and difficulties to be acknowledged.

Selecting and studying the record to be discussed

The student should know in advance of the supervisory session whether he is to choose the record to be discussed, or whether his supervisor wants to concentrate on a particular case with which he is working. Often there is no need to give any thought to the choice of the case, since one will present itself naturally as the most interesting or difficult which the student is handling. However, there may be a particular case on which the supervisor wants to focus more of the student's attention, or she may decide that it would be a good exercise of the student to consider his own work and suggest which interview, or total case, he would like to present for discussion. It can be useful if the student sometimes selects an interview with which he was fairly well satisfied, rather than always concentrating on difficult or unsatisfactory pieces of work, for it is as important to analyse and understand what one does well as to try to correct or improve areas of poor performance.

The supervisor will want to consider the possible teaching points in the record. These may relate (a) to more general questions of agency procedures, national policies in the social services, ethical questions, etc., (b) to diagnostic questions relating to the client and his problem, or (c) to the student's actual handling of the situation recorded, the conduct of the case, and steps to be taken. Some points will be relevant for this particular student, whereas others may be inappropriate to his stage of learning, or will already have been considered; some topics the student will probably want to discuss, while there may be others which the supervisor can guess that he will choose to avoid if possible. Having identified possible teaching points, the supervisor has to consider whether there are certain aspects which she wants to emphasise for this student, or whether all the teaching points are of equal interest, and she will leave it to the student to choose where he would like to begin the discussion.

The supervisor also has to consider the situation from the student's point of view, if she is going to be able to help him to make the best use of the discussion period.

The student may have handed in a case about which he can feel quite pleased, and glad to be able to demonstrate some good work to his supervisor: on the other hand, the case record may show that he made some mistakes, or seemed to achieve nothing, in which case he may be dissatisfied or depressed about his work with the client, and perhaps reluctant to reveal what he regards as poor performance to his supervisor. This is not to suggest that students try to hide their mistakes, and avoid discussion of areas of difficulty. They are mostly eager to improve their understanding and skill by discussion of their work, but at certain points they may need some courage to do it. A supervisor who is aware of the student's possible feelings in the situation, may want to make some acknowledgement of this at the beginning of the supervision session, or to give the student an opportunity to say something about his reactions.

Teaching points

For the sake of clarity, these will be divided into the three main categories suggested above, but in considering an actual record, the divisions are less clear, and often the different issues to be discussed cannot be kept entirely separate. However, it is helpful to a student if there is a definite focus to the discussion.

1. *General topics.* Under this rather vague heading are included all the topics which are not unique to the particular case under discussion, or directly concerned with the student's casework with the client. Questions of policy, national, local or agency; relationships between different branches of the social services, gaps, and areas of overlapping; legal aspects of social work, and moral issues, organisation and administration within the agency itself –

all these are areas of interest for social workers, and matters with which they should be concerned. Some students find the wider aspects of social work of particular interest, and are happy to discuss, for example, the reorganisation of the social services, or the need for reforms in social security provision to meet the needs of certain underprivileged groups, whereas others are much more interested in the psychopathology of an individual client, or their own reactions and learning. The daily job is vitally important, but so are the issues of policy and administration, 'if social workers are not to be willing accessories to what Beatrice Webb referred to as "pulling people out of the swamp when they should be draining it" '.[1]

Social work students are also increasingly being required to study the structure of organisations, and the process of administration in the social work services. Field work placements provide experience of a live situation, in which the student can apply his theoretical knowledge to the understanding of a specific organisation and its administration, in the same way as he tests out the casework teaching in the classroom against his experience with his own clients. For example, a student in the Children's Department must learn the day-to-day work of a Child Care Officer: taking children into care, selecting foster homes, supervising adoption placements and so on. He must also study the organisation in which he is working, its structure, its internal functioning, and its relationships with the other organisations with which it must co-operate and upon which it is therefore partly dependent for the efficient carrying out of its own function. One of the ways in which he can do this is by the discussion of issues of policy and administrative procedures raised by particular cases with which he is working.

Consider the hypothetical example of a student who is

working with a family with several children, the most pressing problem being the threat of eviction from their Council house because of rent arrears. Let us further suppose that the County Borough Children's Department in which he is working operates a scheme to guarantee payment of rent in situations of this kind, where 'preventive' work is being undertaken with the family. Setting aside the particular considerations involved for this family, what are some of the other issues, of a more general nature, which the supervisor and student might discuss?

The student might be asked to consider some fairly basic questions in relation to the *primary* function of a Children's Department. Is it to care for children who are deprived of satisfactory parental care, or is it to prevent children from coming into public care? How can the function of the Children's Department be seen in relation to that of other local authority services? In this instance, to what extent may the department be 'used' by the Housing Department to relieve it of its 'bad debts', and by the Welfare Department to contain the families who might otherwise be seeking 'Part III accommodation'?

Another line of discussion might centre on the administration of the Children's Department itself, as it impinges on the student's work with this case. Suppose that the Children's Officer in person had agreed with the Housing Manager that this family is one with which a Child Care Officer will work intensively, perhaps accepting some responsibility 'to see that the rent is paid'. Does this imply that the person to whom the case is allocated is also being given what almost amounts to a directive to visit weekly, and either collect the rent, or at least inspect the rent book? What degree of freedom does the worker have to examine with the family whether or not they are prepared to use the help being offered – or is he in fact expected to continue visiting unless he is actually told he is not wanted? These may not be easy questions for a supervisor to discuss with a student in her own department, but they are the kind of questions that students do ask, as they must if they are to understand the organisations in which they work, the position of the executive officer at the head of the agency, and the pressures to which he is subject.

Space permits only one other example to illustrate possible general teaching points from a student's case.

> Mrs. B. was separated from her husband, and living with her parents. She had a little girl of a year old, and a second child, a boy, had just been born. There was no suggestion that Mr. B. was not the child's father, yet the wife would not consider reconciliation, and wanted the baby to be placed for adoption. Mr. B. was strongly opposed to the idea. There had been violent quarrelling before the couple parted, and there was a court order in force restraining Mr. B. from going to his wife's home.

This situation could be used as a basis for discussion of the legal aspects of the case: the obligations of a father to maintain his children, the implications of one spouse deserting the home, the grounds on which a husband or wife may make complaint to the magistrates, the law relating to the adoption of children, and who must give consent. The case could also produce a discussion of the moral issue of whether a married couple should be able to 'get rid of' a legitimate child – even if they are living apart. If one parent rejects a child, but the other refuses to allow it to be placed for adoption though unable to care for it, are the legal rights of the parent and the welfare of the child in conflict, and which ought to take precedence?

General topics are important to discuss, both to ensure that a student is clear about specific points in relation to legal and administrative matters, and to give him an opportunity to see his own job as a social worker within the total organisation in which he works, but no student should be allowed to avoid discussion of his own work with clients. Sometimes a student who is reluctant to examine his own performance as a social worker uses topics of general interest to divert attention from areas of discomfort, and while this may be understandable, his ability to help clients will not increase if he does not examine his own performance as a case-worker.

2. *Diagnosis*. (a) *At the beginning*. Before a social worker can take any action, or even formulate a plan, thought must be given to what the problem is, its possible causes and how it may be tackled. Consideration must also be given to the client as a person. How have his past experiences influenced his present attitudes and behaviour? What does *he* feel about the situation he finds himself in now, and how does he think the trouble has come about? What does he want, and how does he think he can best be helped? In some cases a full history is necessary before a diagnosis can be made, but a student may be taught to think methodically about each client he meets, even when the problem is relatively simple. The following example is an illustration of a fairly uncomplicated request for help, from which the student could none the less learn something about diagnosis.

A student working in the Medical Social Worker's department of a general hospital, was asked to see an elderly woman patient who had had a colostomy but was now almost ready for discharge after two months in hospital. The patient lived alone, and wanted the services of a Home Help and the District Nurse. In the course of discussing practical arrangements, the student learned that, although the patient had married children living near enough to visit her, she knew few of her neighbours, having moved to the area only recently. The patient also revealed her fear of the colostomy, and her anxiety about managing it by herself.

The record of the student's second interview begins:

'Saw patient. I told her the District Nurse would be going in. Almost the first thing the patient said was that she did not understand "this bag business". The patient says she knows she worries a lot but has always been the same; said her doctor and children all tell her she worries too much but she cannot help it.'

After two interviews, which were partly concerned with practical arrangements, the student might be helped to summarise what she had learned about the patient and her situation under the following headings:

(1) Factual information.
(2) The patient's attitude and feelings.
(3) An assessment of the total situation.

The student would then be in a position to formulate a tentative plan as to what further help might be needed, having regard to what she knows about the problem, the circumstances, and the patient herself. This is a very simple 'diagnosis' for an early stage of training, but a methodical approach of this kind cannot be introduced too early.

(b) *As a continuing process.* Diagnosis does not just take place at the beginning of a case, but is a continuous accompaniment to work with the client, 'the thinking in problem solving' as Helen Perlman describes it.[2] A supervisor may use a record of an interview at any stage of the casework to help the student to review the position, to consider what the interview has taught him about the client and his situation, and about his capacity to use help. Noel Timms suggests that the term 'diagnosis', as used in social work, often refers to 'both process and product, the path of discovery as well as a description of the arrival-point',[3] and this analysis seems particularly appropriate in the present context. A supervisor must help a student towards the first, and probably tentative, 'arrival-point', and throughout the case will hold him to continuing along 'the path of discovery'.

The following example illustrates a case in which diagnostic material emerged gradually to increase the student's knowledge and understanding of the client and the problem.

Mr. & Mrs. R. were a young couple with four little girls, ranging in age from 4 years to 2 weeks. They were not legally married, as Mr. R. had a wife living elsewhere, and a son whom he had to support. The arrival of the new baby had precipitated a crisis in the family, and the mother had written for help to the local Children's Department, where she was already known, saying that the family could not manage to support a fourth child. The student to whom the case was assigned had found Mrs. R. quite determined that they could not keep the baby, but very reluctant to discuss the matter in any detail, and equally reluctant to have Mr. R. involved directly. However, in the course of several weeks, it was possible to make the following partial diagnosis of the situation.

Mrs. R. seemed an intelligent young woman, who was a devoted mother to her children, and did not herself really want to part with the baby, but felt she must comply with Mr. R.'s wishes. Her frequently repeated statement that it 'did not matter what other people thought' seemed to suggest that in fact she *did* mind what people thought, both about her living with a man who was not her husband, and about her request to have their baby taken into care. Mrs. R. indicated in various ways that she was uncertain of her position, and perhaps afraid that Mr. R. would not stay with the family. She remarked at one point that he had not really wanted children, and did not like girls, 'and I only seem to be able to have girls'.

An interview was arranged in order that the student could meet Mr. R., but when she arrived for the appointment Mr. R. was at work, and Mrs. R. announced that they had decided not to part with the baby after all. Mr. R. had said she could keep the baby 'if that's what you want'. At this interview, Mrs. R. was able to talk more freely about her relationship with Mr. R.

'She discussed with me how difficult she finds it to sit down sometimes, and that when Mr. R. is home in the evenings and he wants her to sit down and talk with him, she finds this difficult. She said, "We haven't any interests in common." I asked what interests she felt they should have in common. She said that they both like music, "but he's much cleverer than I am", and that she often had to pretend to understand what he was talking about when she did not really understand. . . .

She described how surprised and pleased she had been when Mr. R. had prepared the house for her return from hospital after her second confinement, as he would never do anything in the house when she was well. I said that perhaps this had made Mrs. R. feel that he really cared about her. She said, "Yes – he must do, to put up with the children." She looked at me intently and said, "I don't know what I'd do without him – I need him, you see, really need him." We discussed this further, and Mrs. R. said she needs particularly to feel "cared for",

and she really has nobody but Mr. R. to care for her.
Equally, she needs someone to care for. She talked about
Mr. R.'s feelings towards the children – she said he never
offered to help bath the children, and how she had so
often wished that he would. I said that perhaps this
would help Mrs. R. to feel that he saw the children as
his responsibility, and she replied, "Oh, they are my
responsibility, I don't want him to *do* it, but if only he
would offer." '

The material would add to the student's understanding
of the situation, throwing light, as it does, on Mrs. R.'s ideas
about herself as a person, her seeming doubt that she was
worth very much, and her need for reassurance from Mr.
R., which she was often afraid to demand. The student
probably learned from the interview itself, and a subsequent discussion with the supervisor could have been used
to clarify further the student's understanding of Mrs. R.
as a person, and the significance that this understanding
might have for future plans of action. For example, if
further help was to be given to this family, how essential
would it be to include Mr. R.? If this were insisted upon,
how might it affect Mrs. R.?

There would still be many gaps in knowledge about this
situation, and to identify these might help the student to
pursue 'the path of discovery' more purposefully in subsequent interviews. For example, was Mrs. R. really so uncertain of her own worth, or was it only in her relationship
with Mr. R.? Apart from the very obvious and important
fact that Mr. R. provided a home for herself and the
children, what was so important to Mrs. R. in her relationship with her 'husband'? Earlier she had told the student
that he had been in prison since they had started living
together, she herself said they had 'no interests in common',

and she seemed to doubt how much he really cared for her. Yet she had broken off her engagement to another man to live with him, had borne him four children, and she was even prepared to consider parting with her baby, partly at least, because he wished it. Moreover, the record showed she was not entirely alone in the world, being the eldest of a large family, and in frequent and apparently amicable contact with her parents. The answer to these 'diagnostic questions' might not be immediately relevant, but they would almost certainly become so, if work were to continue with this client.

3. *Casework.* (a) *Goals.* At the beginning of any case, the social worker must consider what she hopes to achieve with the client, both immediately and in the long term. This point requires no elaboration here, for it is obvious that the student's aims with each of his clients will have to be discussed with the supervisor at the start. What does have to be borne in mind is the ease with which a sense of direction can be lost in casework, particularly with the client or family, whose life consists of a series of crises. The threat of eviction, pressing debts, the need for immediate arrangements for admission to hospital, or for the care of children, shortage of money or clothes, and a dozen other urgent needs to be met, can cause a student to lose sight of the ultimate objective of his casework. The supervisor will have to hold the student to reviewing his aims periodically, and to considering how far the client is able to understand and agree with them. All students should acquire the habit of reviewing their work regularly, with particular emphasis on the re-defining of objectives.

The supervisor who is discussing with her student the goals of his casework with a particular client or family, has also to bear in mind the stage of learning of the student. The choice of the ultimate goal is determined by the needs and capacities of the client, and the function of the worker's agency, but in deciding how to go about achieving these aims, the skills of the student have to be taken into consideration. As an experienced case-worker, the supervisor may know how she would approach the situation herself, but it may be quite unrealistic to suggest that an inexperienced student should follow the same course. For example, the student may have to go more slowly than she would, and get to know the client better, before he can risk an attempt to discuss the real problem. The supervisor's aim is to help the student find a way of approaching the case, which, although it may be challenging and difficult for him, is not so far beyond his capacities as to paralyse him.

(b) *Assessment of results.* Space permits only a brief reference to the assessment of the results of casework, but it is a topic which should not be ignored in student supervision. There are two aspects to assessment which a student may be required to consider: (*a*) what movement has taken place in the case during the client's contact with the agency and (*b*) to what extent may this be attributed to the social work service given?

The concept of movement, as it is used in social work, is taken to refer to 'changes that take place in clients of social casework during the period when casework services are being furnished'.[4] Movement over a period of time may or may not be the results of casework help. In one case a change in external circumstances, or an apparently spontaneous shift in attitude by one person in a family, may alter the situation considerably for better or for worse. In another case, the movement which the client has been able to make may seem to relate fairly directly to the intervention of the social worker, as the client himself will sometimes acknowledge.

In reviewing progress, in closing or transferring a case, the student should assess what movement has taken place in relation to the position at the time of the last review, or at the beginning of the casework, and at the same time be held to considering to what extent the service he has given to the client may have been responsible for the changes observed. There is no way of proving the results of casework beyond doubt, but this does not absolve the student from attempting some kind of assessment, however tentative.

(c) *The interaction between student and client.* In order to study in detail the way a student handles his interviews, and the interaction between himself and his client, it is essential that the student should keep a process record of the particular interview to be discussed. He will not be ready to produce this kind of record at the very beginning of training, and such discussions will therefore not take place until the student has reached the point of having some understanding of what he is supposed to be doing, and a beginning knowledge of the dynamics of human behaviour. Some familiarity with social work, and enough confidence in his own capacity to do the job, even if at a fairly simple level, will free a student to begin thinking in greater detail about how he himself functions as a social worker. He will need to study the components of the relationship between himself and his client, how they react to each other, what they both say and do in the interview.

In this 'slow motion' study, the student's own strengths and difficulties in relationships will be likely to appear in sharper relief, and can be discussed in relation to specific situations. The greater self-awareness which the student will gain from such discussions will not necessarily result either immediately, or consistently, in changes in behaviour, or in relationships with clients, for it is one thing to know what to do, and quite another to be able to do it. It takes time to translate new understanding into skill.

There are various ways of approaching a discussion which is to be focused on a student's actual performance in an interview; the supervisor may go through the interview from the beginning to the end, discussing points as they arise, or she may select one particular aspect of the student's or the client's behaviour which seems significant, and concentrate on this; or again she may decide to see how aware the student is of the process of the interview, and leave him to choose the points he would like to discuss. The following paragraphs give a few examples of the kind of topics most commonly discussed in supervision.

Communication in the interview is a subject which it is often useful to raise. Did the student really hear what the client was trying to convey? Was he aware not only of the words used, but the way in which they were spoken?

Ferrard and Hunnybun describe the kind of listening which social workers have to achieve, in the following way:

> To be able to listen in this way calls for a quality of repose in the self that makes quiet, reflective listening possible; listening, which in itself gives an assurance of warm interest and concern, yet allows at the same time for attention to be paid to the client's narrative, and those evidences of feeling so often unconsciously revealed by attitude, gesture or tone of voice as he pursues his train of thought.[5]

The full quality of the student's listening may not be evident in the record, but there are often indications of a student failing to grasp something which a client is trying to communicate. This may be shown, for example, by the client continuing to raise a particular topic, either directly or indirectly, and each time the student ignores it. Even in writing the record, the student may not have noticed what was happening. The supervisor will first have to draw the student's attention to what the client seems to have been trying to say, and then get the student to consider what prevented him from hearing the client. It could be due, for instance, to the student's concentration on what he wanted to accomplish in the interview, which blocked his understanding of the client's words and action, or perhaps to a reluctance to pursue the topic, of which he may not even have been aware.

Included in this subject of communication is the actual manner in which the student talks to the client. Young university students particularly sometimes have no idea that they use words and phrases which may be quite out of the ordinary for their clients, and which therefore do not help real communication, even if the client understands the general sense of what is said to him. When a student submits a record which includes jargon, or a lot of rather academic phrases, it is worth asking him to think whether he actually spoke in this way to the client.

Silences are uncomfortable for most people, and for inexperienced students a long silence in an interview is often intolerable. Sudden switches of topic in the record may sometimes mean that the student was frantically trying to fill a silence, and after an interview with a client who was unwilling or unable to talk easily, a student will often himself bring out his own feelings of discomfort and perplexity.

In this matter of communication, as in others, a supervisor may find opportunities to illustrate for the student the points she has raised in relation to his interview with a client, from the relationship which exists between herself and the student. For example, a student who had several times misunderstood information given by clients, also showed very plainly in his relationship with his supervisor that he was sometimes so taken up with his own anxieties, and ideas, that he simply did not hear accurately what the supervisor had said to him. The student tended to deny that he had made mistakes in his casework, but could be helped by seeing that the supervisor's suggestion that he did not seem to listen to his clients was based not only on an interpretation of case records, but also on her own experience of talking to the student.

Feelings, his own and his client's, and how he deals with them need to be discussed with every student. If he responds appropriately and warmly to his client's feelings he probably does so intuitively, and needs to be made conscious of how this helps a client. If he finds some difficulty in handling other people's feelings, he will have to learn how this affects an interview, so that he can make an effort to allow, or even encourage, expressions of feeling. The following excerpt from a discussion shows a supervisor trying to help a student to deal with this difficulty.

Supervisor: Obviously Mrs. D. was pretty upset. How far do you think you helped her to sort out her feelings?

Student: Well, not at all really. She did not seem to want to talk about it at all and every time I got to asking her about her feelings she just turned away and started playing with her little grandchild.

Supervisor: Why do you think she did that?

Student: I thought at the time it was she was afraid I would criticise her or because she was jolly near to tears and would have cried.

Supervisor: Would this have mattered? Sometimes it is a relief to have a good cry.

Student: Yes I know, but I felt very much she did not want to cry with me there and it would have been unkind to have made her.

Supervisor: Yet you seem to have felt frustrated because she bottled up her feelings and would not talk to you.

Student: Whenever I sympathised with her she just turned to the child and did not seem to want to talk about it.

Supervisor: What would have happened had you walked up the path to meet her and said 'Oh poor Mrs. D., what a ghastly time you have had, I am sorry about it'?

Student: I think she might have cried, but I do not think she would have said anything.

Supervisor: Might not the crying have relieved the tension and made it easier for her to talk?

Student: I suppose so, but I think she would have been so ashamed of crying that she would still have been unable to say much.

Supervisor: Would you have been very upset if she had cried?

Student: I think I should have been upset myself because she would have disliked crying in front of me, but I do not think the actual expression of emotion would have upset me.

It may seem that the supervisor was pressing this student rather hard, but later on the record reveals that this particular difficulty was not a new one, and there had been several preceding discussions about the same subject. Many students do find difficulty with the expression of feeling, sometimes only in certain areas. In the example just given, the discussion related to a client's distress which the student had been unable to bring out, but another situation might be concerned with a client's guilty or hostile feelings.

Sometimes a student sees for himself the parts of the interview which he might have handled differently, as he writes it down. On other occasions he may be quite unaware of the possible significance of his own or the client's behaviour, and discuss the interview purely in terms of what actually took place, without perhaps recognising that communication was taking place simultaneously at different levels, and that unconscious factors would also have had their influences in the process of the interview. It is the supervisor's task to help the student look more closely at the dynamics of the interview, to deepen his awareness of the ways in which both he and the client used the interview situation.

No matter which type of teaching point is selected, the supervisor must help the student to relate his theoretical knowledge to the case he is dealing with. Even when fieldwork placements are concurrent with theoretical teaching, the student will often need help in relating the two parts of the course. The academic teachers may, for their part, require the students to bring their fieldwork experience to the classroom to illustrate theory from specific situations, and the fieldwork supervisor has also to require the student to draw on his theory to help him understand his clients, and how they may best be helped. The academic teachers and fieldwork supervisors see the course as a whole, but for the student it may often feel fragmented when he is in the midst of it, and constant cross-reference is necessary to help him to integrate his learning.

REFERENCE

(1) *A Socialist View of Social Work* (pamphlet), Social Workers' Group of the Socialist Medical Association, 1965.

(2) PERLMAN, HELEN. *Social Casework: A Problem-solving Process*, University of Chicago Press, 1957, Chapter XI, p. 164.

(3) TIMMS, NOEL. *Social Casework: Principles and Practice*, Routledge and Kegan Paul, 1964, p. 78.

(4) HUNT, J. MCV. and KOGAN, LEONARD S. *Measuring results in Social Casework*, Family Service Association of America, New York, 1950, p. 6.

(5) FERRARD, M. G. and HUNNYBUN, N. K. *The Caseworker's Use of Relationships*, Tavistock Publications, 1962, p. 32.

VII

Assessing the student's work

At the end of each field work placement, however long or short, some written assessment is made of the student's progress and performance. It is generally requested by the university's field work organiser, or the course tutor, in the case of professional training courses, that the contents of the document be discussed with the student before he leaves the agency. Students, supervisors, and academic teaching staff will all be able to quote examples from their own experience, where this did not in fact happen, and the student either remained for ever ignorant of the contents of his field work report, or else was made aware of it only after he had returned to the university or college. If he were in general agreement with the supervisor's comments, the situation at least did him no harm, but if his opinions were in conflict with the supervisor's assessment of his performance, the situation was an unfortunate one; the student had no opportunity to put his point of view to the supervisor, or to question her interpretation of the situation, and the resulting sense of being a victim of injustice was very real, often vividly recalled years later, when the course had been successfully completed, and the student well established in employment.

There are plenty of reasons why it may be difficult to discuss a student's report: the supervisor may have been too busy to draft it before the student's placement ended, the student himself may not have been anxious for a discussion, or the supervisor may have been reluctant to face the student directly with criticisms, which could be discouraging, or with which he might not agree. Some difficulties may be unavoidable, but the underlying reluctance to discuss an assessment, which is still sometimes present, perhaps arises, at least in part, from a failure to understand the purpose of the report.

Fieldwork reports are ultimately used as part of the overall assessment of the student's performance for the award of the qualification at the end of the course, but this is not their sole purpose, and they are not written purely for the benefit of the tutors. The immediate purpose of any fieldwork assessment is to further the student's learning, and unless it is discussed with him, this purpose is lost. In all but very brief observational placements, the content of the final assessment should not come as a surprise to the student, but should be in the nature of a summing up, a drawing together of the topics which he and his supervisor have been discussing together in the course of the placement. Good supervisory teaching will have made the student aware of his particular strengths and his areas of difficulty, long before the end of the placement, for evaluation of performance is integral to the teaching of a skill. The supervisor is continually assessing the student's performance in order to help him become conscious of what he does, and to learn to improve his skills.

A further point in relation to the student's learning is that an evaluation is not merely an assessment of present performance, but is also a review of progress since the beginning of the placement (or the last evaluation). This

is an aspect which should not be neglected, for it is important for the student to get a sense of how far he has moved
and what he has learned over a given period of time – some
things he will be perfectly aware of, but there may be other
areas of change which he has not noticed.

The evaluation should also be used as a 'springboard'
for further learning, whether in the next period of fieldwork, or in a job. Student and supervisor should together
define the areas of work on which the student wants to
concentrate special attention and effort, and if necessary,
note any particular type of work in which the student needs
experience, so that the next supervisor may be aware of
the student's educational needs from the start.

The evaluation discussion

This will take place at the end of every placement, but
where the placement is a long one, there may also be an
interim evaluation. The discussion is best carried out in two
stages; the main discussion taking place before the written
evaluation is finally drafted, and a second shorter one, when
the document has actually been written. This would ensure
that the student's evaluation is not pushed in at the last
minute before he leaves the agency, but will be regarded as
part of the supervisory teaching, and given adequate time
and attention. It also ensures that, if there are areas of dis-
agreement between supervisor and student, there is time
to think about these, and return to the discussion later, so
that the final written document is, as far as possible, an
agreed statement.

An evaluation discussion should be a joint appraisal of
the student's progress and performance, what he has
learned, what he now knows, and what he can do. It should
not only be the supervisor's assessment of the student's

work, nor, as has occasionally happened, should it rely so heavily on the student's contribution that he feels as if his supervisor has scarcely participated in the assessment. It has the best chance of being a shared discussion if both supervisor *and* student have spent time preparing for it, and if both know the general areas of the student's learning and performance which will be considered. Usually the headings under which the written evaluation is to be set out provide the most convenient framework for the discussion, and the student may be asked to consider his performance under each heading, attempting to assess the areas of strength and weakness, and reviewing what he has learned during the placement.

The following extract from a supervisor's notes of an interim evaluation discussion with a student undergoing professional training will serve as an illustration :

In discussing Miss Garrett's ability to use her theoretical knowledge, I made the comment that she made use of her knowledge when discussing and planning her work, but that sometimes it seemed to confuse her thinking rather than clarify it. It seemed to me that she was perhaps not yet sure enough of her learning to be able to weigh up the different factors involved, and to come out with a composite picture. To this Miss Garrett agreed, saying that she realised her inability to co-ordinate the different aspects of theoretical learning, and to look at the situation as a whole; at present she was looking at a situation in pieces, and could not get an overall view.

Further on in the same record the discussion turned to a consideration of the student's ability to accept and use the function of the agency.

My comment on this point was that Miss Garrett seemed

to have found it hard at first to work in an agency with a very clearly defined function, but that I thought she had begun to see that limitations imposed by function could be helpful, and not only restrictive. Miss Garrett responded with feeling. When I seemed to be restricting and limiting her in her work with clients she became very angry with me – surely I had realised this? I said that I had known she was angry on one or two occasions, and recalled a recent situation when this had happened, which we then discussed.

This record suggests that the student had thought about the discussion beforehand, and her responses to the supervisor's comments give the impression that she knew fairly clearly what she felt and what she wanted to say. The student's contributions also suggest that the student/ supervisor relationship was such that a free exchange of views was possible, as for example when the student told the supervisor how angry she sometimes felt. It might have been better if the supervisor had recognised the student's anger at the time, but as she had not done so, the evaluation discussion gave the student an opportunity to bring out her negative feelings.

If there is a good working relationship between a supervisor and a student, both parties can more easily be critical without too great anxiety about the consequences. A supervisor often finds it difficult to criticise openly, and as a result, may so dilute what she wants to convey to the student that he fails to understand the implication. If the criticism is then more baldly stated in the written evaluation, it can come as a shock to the student, who may even deny that the point was ever discussed with him. If a supportive and helpful relationship with the student has been established, it will not be destroyed by critical comments which are justified, but will support the student and help him to use them to further his learning.

Some students may be confident enough to express negative feelings, or to be critical of something a supervisor has done or said, but for the majority it is a new experience to discover that it is permissible to behave thus in a relationship with a teacher. All students criticise and complain sometimes about those who teach them, but not always face to face, and fieldwork supervisors have to make it clear either explicitly or implicitly that there is no taboo on discussions of the student/supervisor relationship. This is not to imply that the supervisor will necessarily alter her approach if the student is critical, but if the student is free to talk about how he feels, he is less likely to resist the supervisor's efforts to help him to learn.

The scope of an evaluation

The areas of performance to be assessed will differ according to the stage of training the student has reached but, broadly speaking, will in each case be concerned with skills, the application of theoretical knowledge, and attitudes. The evaluation is an assessment of the student's fieldwork, and only an assessment of him as a person, in so far as his personal qualities aid or hinder his performance as a social worker.

1. *Early placements.* Observational placements, and the shorter introductory casework placements, do not provide the opportunity for a student to learn casework skills as such, although he will begin to make contact with clients on his own, and perhaps to share the work on a case with the supervisor. The headings under which the student's performance is assessed are, therefore, usually of a fairly general nature, but still relate to the application of

knowledge, to skills, and to attitudes. The extent of the student's knowledge at this early stage of training is to some extent reflected in, for example, his capacity to grasp the function of the agency, and its administrative procedures, which he will know in theory but will not have observed before in action. His potential skills will be considered in terms of his ability to make relationships, his power of observation, his ability to expresss himself on paper, and so on, while his attitudes may be shown, among other things, by his response to criticism, his willingness to take appropriate responsibility, and his capacity for disinterested understanding.

2. *Professional placements.* The assessment of students at the stage of professional training will relate more specifically to the student's knowledge in certain areas, and his ability to apply it; to the level of his skill, as against the standard required for professional practice; and to his acceptance of the role of a professional social worker. These three areas are all so closely interrelated, that it is difficult to consider them separately, as supervisors often find when attempting to write an evaluation under the headings given by a course.

The knowledge which a student must be able to apply in practice will be in three main areas. First, he must be able to draw appropriately on his knowledge of dynamic psychology and sociology, to help himself to understand his clients, their behaviour, and their difficulties. In certain cases he will also be required to apply what he has been taught about physical and mental illness, and to distinguish between 'normal' and 'abnormal' behaviour and reactions.

Second, he must be able to apply his knowledge of social work method. As a professionally trained social worker, he must be able to understand his work in specific situations in terms of general principles. He will also need an extensive knowledge of the services and resources within the community, and how to use these for the benefit of his clients.

Third, a student must be able to use his knowledge of the law, of the history and administrative structure of the agency, and of organisational theory, in understanding the way in which the agency's service is administered. He must be able to see the function of the social work service within the total organisation, whether it be a probation office, a hospital, or a local authority service.

The skills which a student must acquire in order to qualify as a professional social worker need not be enumerated again here, for the learning and teaching of them has been the central theme of this book, but in a discussion of assessment, some reference to standards of performance cannot be avoided. This is an extremely difficult question, because it seems as if, in present circumstances, there can be no *one* minimum standard of performance which all students should reach in order to qualify as professional social workers. The very fact that courses are of varying lengths, and that, for example, mature students can train for the probation service in one year, but the same students would have to train for two years if they wished to qualify for the child care service, creates a situation of such illogicality that any definition of the minimum standard of performance required of *all* trained social workers must be meaningless.

The assessment of attitudes is of course bound up with the assessment of skills, as for example in the heading in most evaluations which relates to the student's relationship with colleagues and other professional workers. The type of heading which refers to the student's movement towards accepting the role of a professional social worker relates even more specifically to attitudes, if it is taken to include the degree to which the student is identified with the profession, and is prepared to abide by its accepted ethical standards.

The written document

This must be the responsibility of the supervisor, and opinions vary as to whether the student should be given the document to read. A student who has had a full and frank discussion with his supervisor, may not be particularly interested in reading the written document, and some actually prefer not to do so. Others are uneasy if they do not read it.

Whatever decisions are made in individual situations, the supervisor has to keep in mind her responsibilities to the course as well as to the student. The evaluation is written at the request of the course tutor, and a supervisor must give an honest assessment of the student's performance, even when there is a risk of its discouraging the student.

Occasionally a student will ask to have a copy of his evaluation to keep. Before a supervisor agrees to this, the course tutor should be consulted, since the written document does, in a sense, belong to the educational body which has placed the student for his fieldwork training.

The handling of the written evaluation should cause no problems if there are good relationships between the three people concerned: course tutor, supervisor and student. Course tutor and supervisor are both concerned with the student's professional education, and must be able to discuss his progress freely. The student is bound to be anxious when he knows he is being discussed, but he should feel confident that the teachers concerned with both aspects of his training are honestly seeking to provide him with the best opportunities for learning. For his part, the student should feel free to talk to the course tutor about his field-work supervisor, or to the supervisor about the tutor, without feeling that he is being disloyal to either, or that he may be creating difficulties between them.

The academic tutor and the evaluation

Most courses list the areas of the student's performance which they would like the supervisor to assess, and it is helpful if the written document follows the headings given fairly closely. This ensures that the assessment really does cover all aspects of the student's work, and also that there is some degree of standardisation for fieldwork assessments throughout the course. The supervisor is usually asked to include short notes on particular cases or situations which the student has handled, which will illustrate points made in the evaluation. For example, a student who has found it difficult to take the initiative with his clients, may have reached a point during the placement where he has been able to risk facing a particular client with the reality of a difficult situation, and has found that this has been helpful to the client. A general statement of the student's progress in this area, illustrated by short notes about the situation which helped him to learn the particular point, supports and clarifies the supervisor's assessment of his progress.

Once the evaluation reaches the course tutor, it may be used to discuss with the student his overall progress on the course, and it will certainly form part of the final assessment for the award of the qualification. This sometimes worries supervisors, especially if they have been supervising a student who does not seem to have made much progress. The supervisor may feel she is going to be the cause of the student's total failure on the course, and will almost certainly wonder whether she is at least partly to blame for his poor progress.

This is always a difficult situation, but the supervisor has to bear in mind that the course tutors and examiners must take ultimate responsibility for passing or failing students, and that there is more than one fieldwork supervisor's assessment for each student. On the other hand, she also has to accept that the fieldwork supervisors are the only people who are in a position to know the standard of a student's work, and she will fail in her responsibility as a supervisor if she does not provide as objective and honest an assessment as she can. For their own and their clients' sakes, some students cannot be allowed to qualify.

Conclusion

It would be a pity to end by considering failure. Students are carefully selected for courses of professional training, and although there are bound to be occasional mistakes, the majority of social work students have chosen a career for which they are suited, and they complete their courses quite successfully. Training in this field does make more than ordinary demands on the students, and the ability of the majority to respond, to learn new skills, and to develop as people, during a relatively short space of time, is an encouraging indication of the quality of the entrants to professional social work.

Further reading

Literature on the subject of field work supervision is limited, and in this country most of the published material is to be found in articles and pamphlets. The list of suggestions for further reading which follows is by no means exhaustive, but will enable the reader to pursue some of the topics which have been touched upon briefly in this book. The first section refers to material concerned with education for social work generally, and includes some books and articles more specifically about field work. The second section contains articles and pamphlets which focus more on the task of the field work supervisor.

Section I

(1) DEWEY, JOHN *Experience and Education*, Macmillan, New York, 1938.
(2) HOWARTH, ELIZABETH 'The Objectives of Professional Training', *Accord*, Vol. XI, No. 1, 1966.
(3) STEVENSON, OLIVE 'The Skills of Supervision – a Study of Teaching Method', in *New Thinking for Changing Needs*, Association of Social Workers, 1963.
(4) TOWLE, CHARLOTTE *The Learner in Education for the Professions As Seen in Education for Social Work*, University of Chicago Press, 1954.

(5) OAKESHOTT, M. 'The Study of "Politics" in a University' in *Rationalism in Politics* and other essays, Methuen, 1962.
(6) ROBINSON, VIRGINIA P. (Ed.) *Training for Skill in Social Case Work*, University of Pennyslvania Press, 1942.
(7) BROWN, CLEMENT S. and GLOYNE, E. R. *The Field Training of Social Workers*, Allen and Unwin, 1966.

Space permits only a brief comment on some of this material. John Dewey's philosophy of education is a congenial one for social work, and readers who are interested in applying educational theory to teaching in social work will find both his book, and Olive Stevenson's paper, stimulating and interesting. Charlotte Towle's book is a standard work on the subject of social work education, and repays careful study, but for practical purposes, most field work teachers will probably find it too long and too detailed.

Section II

(1) GARRETT, ANNETTE 'Learning Through Supervision', *Smith College Studies in Social Work*, Vol. XXIV, No. 2, February 1954.
(2) *Report of the Seminar on Supervision*, Association of Social Workers, 1955.
(3) HOWARTH, ELIZABETH 'An Introduction to Casework Supervision', *Case Conference*, Vol. 8, No. 6, November 1961.
(4) DEED, D. M. 'Danger of Stereotypes in Student Supervision', *Case Conference*, Vol. 9, No. 1, May 1962.
(5) AUSTIN, LUCILLE N. 'Basic Principles of Supervision', December 1952, *Social Casework*. Reprinted in *Techniques of Student and Staff Supervision*. New York Family Service Association of America.
(6) ZETZEL, ELIZABETH R. 'The Dynamic Basis of Supervision', April 1953, *Social Casework*. Reprinted in *Techniques of Student and Staff Supervision*. New York Family Service Association of America.
(7) STEVENSON, OLIVE 'Process Records', *Accord*, Vol. VIII, No. 2, Winter 1962–3.
(8) HEYWOOD, JEAN S. *An Introduction to Teaching Casework Skills*, Routledge and Kegan Paul, 1964.

All the material referred to in Section II is in the form of articles, except for Jean Heywood's and Annette Garrett's books, and the A.S.W. pamphlet. The other articles contained in the F.S.A.A.'s collection of eleven are also worth reading, although some are concerned with staff, not student supervision. For supervisors who are new to the job, Elizabeth Howarth's article is especially useful, and the A.S.W. pamphlet will also repay study.

Date Due

FEB

OCT 22 '95

Demco 293-5